Maybugs
and
Mortality

A different perspective on living and ageing

Phoebe Caldwell

Maybugs and Mortality
A different perspective on living and ageing

© Pavilion Publishing and Media

Published by:
Pavilion Publishing and Media Ltd
Blue Sky Offices
25 Cecil Pashley Way
Shoreham by Sea
West Sussex
BN43 5FF
Tel: 01273 434 943
Fax: 01273 227 308
Email: info@pavpub.com

Published 2019

ISBN: 978-1-912755-21-9

Pavilion Publishing and Media is a leading publisher of books, training materials and digital content in mental health, social care and allied fields. Pavilion and its imprints offer must-have knowledge and innovative learning solutions underpinned by sound research and professional values.

Editor: Phoebe Caldwell
Production editor: Mike Benge, Pavilion Publishing and Media Ltd.
Cover design: Phil Morash, Pavilion Publishing and Media Ltd.
Page layout and typesetting: Emma Dawe, Pavilion Publishing and Media Ltd.
Printing: CMP Digital Print Solutions

'Despite their small size, insects do in certain areas, render human existence precarious if not impracticable. Even by what may be termed, their own legitimate activities, they destroy or interfere with and immense amount of human effort.'

Eltringham H (1933) *The Senses of Insects*. Methuen Monograph.

Contents

Chapter 1: Tandem

Maybugs and Mortality is about an accidental encounter and subsequent relationship; a lopsided alignment, since at the time my maybug/cockchafer was staggering on its last six legs. But even though clearly on its way out, our meeting was – and is – important to me, as it made me see myself (in the person of Everyman/Everywoman) from a different angle. For the last two years, my maybug has lived on as my companion, and this book is a personal, intimate and in places autobiographical yet hopefully light-hearted exploration of the latter half of our life cycles, with forays into our respective youths.

Together we have visited such comparative landscapes as what it feels like to walk round corseted by an external cuirass rather than supported by an internal ramrod: the alternatives, say, between ice cream in a tub and an ice-lolly with a stick up its middle. Are there psychological consequences as well as physical differences? Rather surprisingly, we shall attend a 14th century Ecclesiastic Court in Avignon and listen to Kafka's disquieting sci-fi story of a man who wakes up one morning to discover he has turned into a beetle. We shall touch on life in a grey world, watch emotions bob up and down and lap the far shores of Consciousness and Self-Awareness. Drawing on my experience of autism we shall examine what we mean when we talk about boundaries, the difference between 'me' and 'not me', and the need to reach out beyond ourselves in order to find confirmation and understanding – before returning to earth via a tea-break at the uncomfortably named 'Death Café'.

Such diversity has tour-guide problems: it is highly selective. Topics inflate, take the bit between their teeth, which, however fascinating, need to be reined in. And there is a question of style. Reared among academics (mathematicians, engineers and doctors), empiricism papered the walls of my bedroom. Everything requires proof; the fact that such certainty is inevitably outgrown has failed to shake my belief in the veracity of the scientific method.

But somewhere along the line I acquired a familiar – a comedian who sits on my shoulder and whispers irreverent interpretations into my ear. I call him 'Till' (after Till Eulenspiegel, a practical joker of dubious probity and historicity[1]).

The dichotomy between earnest enquiry and fun is difficult to resolve. Psychological research does its best to stifle light-heartedness when we are told that humor stems from 'a benign violation of the way the world ought to be'[2], a definition that falls flat on its face. More to the point, while science is indifferent to the nature of our surroundings, humor wants to snuggle up and tweak the facts; it's looking for a response – and in this sense it is manipulative. Here is a fundamental difference in temperament: attempting to coax the two into bed with each other lapses into a wrestling match between

---

1 Subject of an opera by Richard Strauss, Till could not resist a final despairing one-liner even as he waited on the scaffold with the rope round his neck.

2 Hutchison P (2010) Scientists discover the secret of humor. *The Telegraph* **12 August**.

the sublime and the ridiculous. But before going further, the science in *Maybugs* is as accurate as I can ascertain. Journals have been perused, papers trawled and – although there has been an exponential explosion in research since I graduated more than 60 years ago – at least partially understood. My reason for embracing such a dubious binary strategy is that, although I fell in with the wandering insect by accident, it has led me to new perspectives, to speculate in a different way on what it means to be alive.

Maybugs and Mortality is so bizarre that I feel the need to excuse myself. Told slightly tongue in cheek, it contains little empirical evidence and is more in the nature of a string of ideas. While it flirts with frivolity and is a story that embraces surface textures, it also explores the inner comings and goings of an unlikely relationship. It is like a string of beads. Each bead may have its own colour, shape, weight and luminosity – its own character. The temptation to dally is occasionally irresistible. What is important is the thread that joins them together, which resolves into an enquiry: how does so much of what we understand as 'being alive' get packed into such an unlikely container?

To begin with, why 'a monograph for two'? I hope it will become evident that, while trying to side-step the pot-hole of anthropomorphism, I am using my maybug encounter to explore certain aspects of our shared life-cycles. In this respect we are riding in tandem; journeying together, even if only one of us is doing the pedalling most of the time.

Journeys of any length have a backup team: mine is a lifetime spent working with people on the autistic spectrum. It is from them that I have learned to look at what we mean by 'relationship'. If I have been able to help them engage with a world that is sensorily confusing, they have changed my life. Occasionally I shall borrow their words to throw light on some aspect of my psychological globe-trot.

As I wrote this book I found myself abandoning the formality of 'Cockchafer', in favour of 'the maybug' – and as we became more intimately acquainted, just 'Maybugs', as in, 'Hi there, Maybugs', the nickname of a familiar friend. (When it comes to classification, there will be occasional reference to Melolontha Melolontha.) And while being aware of the immense diversity of insect forms – and since *Maybugs and Mortality* is in no sense an academic treatise – where it is available I shall borrow freely from other insects (some sufficiently distant as to be categorised as 'remote kith' rather than 'kin'), provided they meet the criteria of possessing external support as opposed to a soft boundary with world outside them. My excuse for taking such outrageous liberties with taxonomy is to look at the physical and psychological schism existing between the corseted existence of the insect and the more flexible possibilities of life supported by an internal skeleton – and if possible to clear out some of my own dustier corners along the way.

The cockchafer/maybug, whose ungainly adult form resembles a sarcophagus on wheels, is squat, brown, hairy and tessellated, with a row of what appear to be triangular white tiles down each side. It emerges in May and has attracted many names. In alphabetical order we have: 'Bracken Clock',

'Boomerbug', 'Bummler', 'Chovy', 'Cob-worm', 'Dorrs', 'Dumbledarey', 'Humbuz', 'June Bug' (shifting a month, and mainly in America), 'Kittywitch', 'Billywitch', 'May-bittle', 'Midsummer Dor', 'Mitchamador', 'Oak-wib', 'Rookworm', 'Snartlegog', 'Spang beetle', 'Tom beedel' and 'Chwilen y bwm' (to the Welsh). Perhaps my favourite is 'Doodlebug', since the insect's slow and noisy flight conflates with the bogeyman of my childhood – Hitler's penultimate weapon, the V1, that chugged its way across the English Channel and was designed to bring Britain to her knees. Until recently I had a light-weight metal fragment of the air intake of a doodlebug on my desk which I had swapped with my cousin for a couple of sweets. Last year I gave it to my grandson who, at the time, was working on the mathematics of the nose cone of a rocket to Mars, and whether or not it would burn up.

It is difficult to pass by a maybug; they are large and not immediately attractive. They bang on windows and pursue their flight-paths irrespective of interruption. And while I can marvel at their jointed construction (a combination of rigidity and flexibility and the ingenuity of their wing hinges), it is not easy to engage emotionally with an armour-plated 'other' that cannot reciprocate. There is no affective orifice in that chitinous wall: I cannot find my way into an insectile heart.

While I do not think I actually like insects, maybugs come with a wealth of stories – if the flight path is erratic, the destination is fascinating. And if I have not entirely set aside distaste, I have learned respect and, at times, felt an odd affection for my fellow traveller.

Chapter 2: Encounter

Assault by a maybug is like being struck by a tank stuck in first gear. While it might seem that the impact is due to the creature's poor navigational skills, in practice the clumsy creature knows exactly where it is going. It is locked onto its destination but lacks flexibility when it comes to circumnavigating obstacles. Picking itself up after a collision, it will resume its original route.

I must have been about seven at the time of my first encounter. Perhaps it was surprise that temporarily bounced me off balance: the impact was unexpectedly hefty and ground zero is still demarcated by a sensory crater slightly to the right of a chicken pox scar in the middle of my forehead. Somehow, one does not expect an insect to pack such a powerful punch.

Nearly 80 years on, these reflections surface as I pause to support myself against a wall that borders the upper lane beneath the overhanging Castlebergh Rock. By my feet, a heavily armoured maybug is heaving his (or her) unlovely body across the setts at a rate of progress which makes it unlikely it will reach the precarious safety offered by the other side of the lane before June. I am torn between the notion that I should assist this journey and the instinct that I should not interfere with destiny. The latter wins and I turn away from the struggle, lean over the wall and rest my chin on the topping stones while considering where I live.

Deliberately not having had it delivered, I've set out to buy my paper, forcing a daily walk to fetch it from the newsagent and thereby exercising dwindling muscles. Each day, the exact route chosen becomes a matter of honour and self-negotiation, whether to include the climb – or funk it and walk back the along the flat. Weighing in on the steep side is a feeling of virtue, of 'keeping going', of 'not giving in'. Added to which the easy way is extremely dull, crossing an endless car park which, although spruced up recently for the Great Yorkshire Bike Race, has quickly relapsed into its familiar role as overnight stopover for charity minibuses; the benevolence of its donors and disability of its passengers boldly splashed on their sides.

Having chosen the upper route, I am eye-level to assorted chimney pots. Below me, the small market town of Settle falls away towards the young River Ribble, where it swaps its limestone nursery for an embankment of old mills, now converted into expensive-looking flats. Over across the valley, the hills of the distant Forest of Bowland are bare, not a tree to be seen, naked as a nursing mother's breast.

The lane up from Market Square is steep. Its gradient feels almost vertical, like climbing a ladder. Rung by rung, I pass cottages on either side of the narrow road. Utilitarian names stretch back to a time when Settle was an important pack-horse ford over the Ribble: 'The Old Brewhouse', 'The Well', 'The Old Warehouse', 'Forge Cottage', 'Old Stables', 'The Dreyhouse' (possibly a different spelling of dray, a cart), and 'Chandlers Cottage', presumably an old name for a general ironmonger rather than its now more common usage of ship's suppliers. 'Junction Lodge' is an exceptionally slim house pinned between two divergent lanes (narrow as the angle between my third and fourth finger and holding its breath). Its owner is leaning over her balcony. She tells me there was a lot of tanning in the area and points to her neighbour's cottage, 'Currier Cottage' (curriers prepared leather after tanning). 'The Tannery' itself is a Grade Two listed building further up the hill in Commercial Street, backing onto the Green, looking out over the fields and hills behind.

At first I suppose that the commercial centre of gravity has shifted downhill to its present location around the Market Place – but further investigation reveals that the processes of curing hides smelled so appalling that tanneries were normally to be found on the edge of towns. After washing the skins in water, the hair was removed by soaking them in urine, or allowing them to putrefy. Pigeon or dog faeces was pounded into the skins to soften them. Nothing was wasted in this eco-friendly but foul-smelling process. Piss-pots on the corners of the street collected the cottagers' urine. Children were employed to collect dung[3].

Carrie, who I meet by chance walking her dog, identifies 'The Tannery' as the cottage with three chimney pots, now privately owned. She tells me her husband is the gardener. A stream that runs down by the garden would have provided water for cleaning the hides. Soft fruit, gooseberries and raspberries grow in the filled-in but still fertile soaking pits: next door is a huge stone slab now used for picnics, originally a base for scraping the hair from the skins. Nearby is a small cottage called 'Salt Pie', probably referring to the storage barn for salt used in curing the hides.

Zigzagging back down to the lower lane, the front entrance to Currier Cottage has a contemporary plaque with a welcome for the visitor – 'Pax intrantibus. Salve exeuntibus. Benedictus Habitatibus' – and a translation in smaller letters for those of us whose Latin is shaky: 'Peace be on those who come, God Speed those who depart, Blessings on those who dwell herein'.

Pausing to absorb such spiritual generosity, my eye falls on an ancient milestone set into the wall, which now tells me precisely where I am – suspended on an invisible string 263 miles west of London and 17 miles east of Kirby Lonsdale. It is at Kirby that another river, the Lune, makes its break from the Dales, flowing southwards through a spectacular valley on its way to Lancaster. Recommended for outstanding beauty by William Wordsworth in his *Guide to the Lakes*[4], the Lune valley is equally famous in our family as the site where my son-in-law did his best to drown a squad of paratroopers by ramming their canoe into a sand bank.

However it's not just me standing here, Maybugs is here too. Our chance meeting is where this story begins, the epicentre of a shift in the way I regard the fault line between what is 'me' and 'not me'.

I am not an entomologist – and if my current preoccupation with cockchafers and their insect relatives may be seen to be eccentric, even obsessional, it stems

---

3 https//en.wikipedia.org/wiki/Tanning_leather
4 *The Illustrated Guide to the Lakes* (1984) Exeter: Webb & Bower.

from curiosity acting as a spring-board for speculation. Both bug and I are alive and both of us have to deal with the environment in which we find ourselves. Although we inhabit selective niches, to some extent we overlap. How widely have the exigencies of evolution pushed us in one direction or another? How closely do we resemble each other and how far have we drifted apart?

Leaving my exhausted maybug to its fate as I turn for home, she or he is already busy imprinting his or her footprints into my consciousness as well as knocking at the walls of my conscience. So when I get home I sit down and reach for my mouse and set off online. I want to know more.

Despite his or her unprepossessing body, full on face to face, the expression of a cockchafer is not unappealing, somewhat like a whimsical meercat sporting a couple of large fascinators; antennae deeply divided into separate petals, six on each side of the head for the female and seven for the male. While hers may or may not be purely decorative (but are more probably the site for her sense of smell), his are specialised, able to detect the come-hither pheromones sent out by a potential mate.

The reason for my gender hesitation is that sexing a cockchafer is not necessarily about an ability or inability to count up to ten. In the eyeball-to-eyeball, blown-up picture that is my guide, the right antenna has six divisions and the left, seven[5]. Does this indicate bisexuality, trans-sexuality or, since cannibalism is not unknown among insects, did one flange get nipped off in the ecstasy of coition? A more mundane explanation to such gender asymmetry might be that the antennae, which look like puffed-up six or seven-fingered rubber gloves, could be related to slackness of the muscle surrounding the vase-shaped pump at its base, too exhausted to fully inflate the small finger on one side. I decide to settle for female. But perhaps the critical question is whether or not a puzzled partner will stop to negotiate in mid-mount?

For myself, sell-by-date is approaching; time has become erratic, and idle speculation is a pleasant way of marking the passage of a dimension that is either galloping away over the horizon or has lost its stretch, the intervals between birthdays drooping like old knicker elastic. A resident of the block of flats that is my home (variously named 'Retirement Apartments', 'Sheltered Housing', or, to the irritation of some of its residents, 'Dementia Homes') stands in the car park, shouting, 'I haven't got anything to do'. His complaint bounces off the walls, trails off in a one-way echo: a koan of aloneness with no feedback[6].

So, if I'm not to lapse into dull-eyed sadness and a list of ailments, I need a plan. Memo: keep walking. My eyes fasten on the flag fluttering from its pole at the summit of Castlebergh Crag. Maybe, maybe not, but one day I shall try and reach its dizzy heights. Old age may have given me time, but in the unlikely event that Maybugs, waving her fronded antennae, has succeeded in her crossing without being picked off by a hungry corvid or squashed under the wheels of a car, she will not have long to live. Three to five years as a grub

---

5 https://www.buglife.org.uk/bugs-and-habitats/common-cockchafer

6 A koan is a riddle or puzzle that Zen Buddhists use during meditation to shock the brain into unravelling greater truths about the world and about themselves. The classic example of a Koan is 'the sound of one hand clapping'.

underground (gender orientation not yet visibly differentiated), munching her way through roots of grass or potato, all that time before sexual maturity and then only five weeks left to party.

Unloved, for some unexplained reason, maybugs appear in large swarms every 30 years (or five depending on the source of information). On the other hand, life spans are relative. Set against the age of the universe, 13.772 billion years, with an uncertainty factor of 59 million years, my personal time-scale looks pretty meagre. That is, of course, unless I am prepared to share my brains with a cyborg. Nevertheless, human rather than insect, the story of my body is much the same as yours – we are born, we grow, we lose our innocence (rather earlier these days than in mine), we mature, reproduce, struggle with the realities of our lives, fail, die, or as a friend put it, 'pop our clogs'. Although I doubt if my executors will be dashing off to the pawnbrokers with my somewhat battered sandals.

Whatever the euphemism, mortality is certain and however hard we may try to put it off, death is what happens to us humans and to Maybugs. But even if Maybugs battles on in ignorance, the difference between us is that we humans already know the end of the story.

Nevertheless, the preliminaries – the dwindling and wasting – are rather more obvious when our flesh erodes, than if we had a rigid outer casing. They come as a shock, crystallised by one of my daughters who, looking at my wedding photograph, turned to me in mock surprise, 'What happened?' The primary essential to survival in old age is a sense of humour.

So what did happen to that eager face and blossoming flesh, full of the alchemy of love and fired with potential?

My first old person is a great-aunt, Great Aunt Lil, youngest surviving of seven sisters, living in the gate house to which she had been relegated following an affair with the coachman. She is sitting erect in her kitchen, one arm resting on a scrubbed wooden table, dressed in a long blue cotton dress with a starched white apron and cloth cap hiding her hair. She has the stillness of a Vermeer portrait. In retrospect, I think she may also have heart failure since she is swollen, monumental.

My mother says, 'Kiss your aunt Lil', but since she is unable to bend down, I have to clamber up on her footstool and from thence to the arm of her chair. It feels like scrambling up the slabs of a mountain crag: I am in need of a rope and harness, and even so am only able to manage a dab at her stiff collar. Abseiling the descent in my mother's arms, I am sent into the garden to look at the mulberry tree (laden with fruit and crawling with wasps) and the donkey ('look for the cross on his back'), while family gossip is exchanged.

And then there is Great Uncle George, who comes to stay with us during the war to keep warm and sleep in front of the only fire. Furtive attempts on my part to sneak in and share the warmth are met with, 'Don't go into the sitting room and wake your Uncle George'; a chilly prohibition, mitigated only by the thought of not having to embrace him.

My third encounter with the ravages of decrepitude is when Emma, an elderly friend of my mother's, comes to stay. The weather is sparkling and the tide just right. Kitted out in all-embracing bathing costumes and rubber caps, we ease ourselves off the rickety wooden pier at the edge of the creek. I turn to Emma who is standing in the shallows, looking up and smiling. Flaps of the flesh on her arms are floating in the water, bobbing on the ripples, rafts without substance, weightless as empty plastic bags, almost independent of the limb. I can see her still but the imprint of my memory, borne on a waft of cringe, recoils. Something is clearly amiss.

Eighty-odd years on and here I am. Me. Same contents inside, but the packaging is battered, falling apart. Too late for a makeover, it's my turn for corrugated and empty, papery skin, soil of a dried-out garden that has been allowed to go to seed, warty weeds sprouting and puddles of discoloration spreading across the back of my hands. And due to the great subsidence, the overall picture is comparable to the massive uplift and slippage that embraces the town of Settle, known as the Craven Fault, such bulk as there is, mounted in the wrong places. (At least the Fault is grassed over.) Movement is ponderous and liable to take off in the wrong direction – I dare not turn round too quickly. The younger version was preferable.

But should I want to go back? And, in the other direction, and beyond the salve of rejuvenating ointments and botox, just how far do I want to advance? Lunching with a friend recently and mulling over the state of the world, we joke that we might take one last holiday together on a one-way ticket to Switzerland. Perhaps not yet, but it seems preferable to the prospect of extended deterioration.

Chapter 3: Beetles and guardian angels

It is the day of the Part One Finals Practical examination. I am standing with my year group in a gloomy passage outside the door of the zoology laboratory, waiting to find out which specimen we candidates are to be required to investigate. The glass panel is blocked by a notice, 'Examination – Quiet'; we are unable to see what is in store for us. Courage is oozing like raw haggis out of my toes. The door opens. Hands sweating, we fan out to our benches and stand in front of our dissection boards, to each of which is pinned a large insect, together with an instruction to explore its central nervous system.

My heart sinks. Dissection of insects is the anatomy class that I had missed and never caught up with. I cannot even remember whether their nervous system runs up the front or back. Help, where is it? Caution comes to my rescue and suggests opening this creature up the side is the most likely way in to avoid severing the target.

This is where my guardian angel has already been at work, since by chance (or divine intervention), my specimen is full of nematode worms. Evicting the squatters, I have a quick poke round, unearthing what can only be a nerve cord running, not up the back like mine but up its front, one ganglion to each segment, totally unlike anything I've seen before. At least now I know where to start. Reassured, I raise my hand requesting the invigilator to provide a specimen with vacant possession. From then on it's plain sailing. Forgetting the examination, I probe tapering fibres under a binocular microscope: time slips by as I wander in the segmented beauty of its fan-vaulted tracery.

Five minutes to go and naming the various parts of the creature's anatomy poses a problem, but 'abdominal', 'thoracic' and 'cranial' seem fairly safe adjectives to use, although they omit the interesting bits in the head – it must be obvious to anyone marking the practical that this candidate has absolutely no idea as to how these parts should be labelled.

Second chances always seem to be miraculous; a special dispensation requiring outside intervention, a guardian angel deputised to look after one's special interests. To my knowledge I have only met one: carved into the stone capital of a pillar in a small church in Ewyas Harold, Saint Peter hangs upside on his cross, since the saint did not feel himself worthy to be crucified in the same orientation as his Master. Whether or not one recognises the substantiality of this intermediary with the Divine, it led me to reflect on the desirability of having a companion willing to accompany me through life's more acrobatic intimacies, to be there for me through thick and thin and ultimately to hold my hand as I scramble through the gates of death.

As for gender, although I harbour doubts as to whether my ally is a sexually defined creature, existing archangels are definitely masculine – Gabriel,

Michael, Raphael, and the rather less familiar, Uriel, Saraqael, Raguel and Remiel. And even if my companion is one of the lesser rank, a mere angel, it feels disrespectful to call him 'it'. Addressing this imbalance, like Maybugs, I shall settle for 'her', even if her earthly appearances suggest that gender is not an issue and most of her appearances are male; she adopts whatever disguise is convenient at the time.

Feet on the ground, my angel seems to be as good an explanation for the phenomena of synchronicity as any offered by science, and continues (occasionally) to shift contexts on my behalf in a way that is difficult to reconcile with my patchy belief. But without her, agnosticism does have difficulty in accounting for some of the more unlikely coincidences that surface from time to time.

And if she exists, my guardian angel has been busy, dragging me out of ditches and heaving me over fences. Put it down to luck but such casual rearrangements carry with them a whiff of the supernatural.

She seems well versed in zoology: is it really just a matter of chance that when, short of time, I toss a coin and spend the night before the theory exam immersed in an unread chapter on the symmetry of sea cucumbers and star fish, brittle stars and sea urchins? The next day I turn over the paper and here it is, a question asking for a complete description of the Echinoderms. Carrying quarter of the marks, this is a subject on which I had been completely ignorant the day before yesterday: small stuff, even trivial, but essential in order to progress through Part One, towards that ultimate goal of Bachelor of Science.

My angel's interventions seem arbitrary, 'out of the blue'. Twenty years later, when the direction of my life has changed, I need a workshop in which to build sensory equipment for residents in the local 'Hospital for the Mentally Handicapped' as it was then known – and where I am working as an Occupational Therapy Helper. An unknown man appears at my door, tells me he understands I need a workshop, builds one, fits it out for me over the next three weeks, and then disappears out of my life.

Perhaps one of my guardian's more unlikely visits comes when I am working far from home. I need to find some way of accessing the isolated world of a man who has had an accident that has left him blind, deaf and angry – so angry he has turned his back on the world, to the extent that he has ended up in a ward for people with profound disabilities. I am told there is nowhere else that is sufficiently staffed to contain his hostility[7].

It occurs to me that what I need is an alphabet with robust letters. (Fridge magnets are too small for his large hands.) By chance I sit down at supper next to the manager of a timber factory, who is very proud of the new cutting machine he has just installed. He tells me that it will tailor any shape out of MDF. I bet him it can't do alphabets. Next week I have three. The letters are three and a half inches high; it only remains to make suitable racks to hold them. Starting with 'NO' and 'OK' (OK on the advice of a psychologist in that it may be easier to recognise), there is almost immediately an extremely irritated demand for 'YES'.

7 Caldwell P (2016) *Driving South to Inverness*. Pavilion Publishing & Media.

One of the characteristics of my guardian angel is that she does not linger; she appears without announcement, fixes what is necessary and is off without even pausing to say goodbye.

There are times when coincidence feels like an obstacle course in which mirage hazards melt away almost before they appear on the horizon, as if there really is some other controlling hand at work. Maybe it's just down to odds?

But there are some synchronisms that are so improbable that, rather than chance, it seems more logical to ascribe them to a guardian angel, even a stone angel standing on his head in a Herefordshire chapel. In the medieval mystery play, 'Everyman', the only creature able to accompany the protagonist into the grave is 'Good Works'. Even if I am not quite convinced of the corporality of my guardian angel, I am more comfortable with the idea of their semi-human interventions than to the bleakness of wrestling with a totally indifferent environment, one that simply does not care about me. (Me being singularly important, I'm the only one I've got.)

And while I'm alive, the seemingly ridiculous idea of a delightful companion adjusting the world to my long-term requirements breeds optimism and is more fun than struggling on my own. On the other hand, she can be fickle and she really does need to explain her absences when I am desperate for supernatural intervention to rearrange the circumstances of my life.

And then there is the awkward question, how is she going to juggle my needs into the jigsaw requirements of others? Preferential treatment seems unfair but she cannot please everyone. The picture that emerges is of angels jostling for attention at the head of the divine queue, rather than choirs clutching harps and singing in unison. Projecting my 'me first' biological struggle for existence into another dimension I shall shift the guilt – and blame the angel for failure: she was busy elsewhere when needed.

Chapter 4: Cherry-picking history

Back to beetles: there are around 30,000 different species of them. Ten percent of these are scarabs, including Maybugs, whose most famous first cousin is the dung beetle (Scarabaeus viettei) and from whose lifecycle I shall extrapolate, since its bizarre habits have attracted attention from the earliest times. The most obvious behaviour of the scarab is it that of rolling large chunks of dung into a ball and, facing backwards, pushing it round with its back legs.

Interpretations of this odd behaviour vary. Plutarch comments that the Egyptians thought that only the males behaved in this way, inseminating the dung and imitating the path of the sun as it went down in the west and rose in the east in the morning[8]. Closer observation suggests that the male and female usually work together. She drops her eggs on the ground and then covers them in dung on which the larvae will feast. As they push the soft ball over the sand in search of a suitable place to bury it, it collects sand and hardens, sometimes to the size of the beetle itself[9].

An alternative account includes the direction finding behaviour associated with this strenuous courtship: 'scarabaeus' feeds exclusively on dung, diving into pats and rolling chunks into balls, using its back pair of legs as shovels. When it has collected sufficient dung to make a large ball, 'it climbs on top of it, cleans its eyes, stretches out its head, wriggles its body from side to side a few times, and performs a little dance'. Far from letting it all hang out, recent research suggests that these exertions are related to direction finding; when it has calibrated its sat-nav, it climbs off and, head down, pushes the ball with its hind legs away from the mother pat, rolling it backwards. Finding a suitable soft site, it scrapes a hole and buries its prize[10]. A Stakhanovite Scarab is able to bury 250 times its weight in dung overnight. Usually it is the male who rolls the ball, but sometimes the female helps, occasionally 'hitching a ride'[11], clinging on precariously since steering backwards over pebbles is erratic and she is in danger of being thrown off, or even squashed.

The bigger the ball the more attractive it is to a potential mate (strong rear legs equates to stamina and good breeding prospects). Arriving at a suitable spot, the female scarab lays her eggs in the buried dung, so when the grubs

---

8 Plutarch, Greek writer (ca AD40-120).

9 Evans EA (1996) 'Ancient Egypt The Sacred Scarab' McClung Museum, University of Tennessee, Knoxville https://mcclungmuseum.utk.edu/1996/01/01/sacred-scarab/

10 Cardiff J (2001) Melolontha Melolontha Common European cockchafer [online]. University of Michigan Museum of Zoology. Available at: http://animaldiversity.org/accounts/Melolontha_melolontha/ccvcv
   fdfd

11 ibid.

hatch they will have plenty of food to eat[12]. Not surprisingly, rival males will fight vigorously (head down, charge and flip each other over in a backward somersault through the air) for possession of a particularly desirable ball, even resorting to deception by assisting a struggling suitor to overcome an obstacle, while waiting for an opportunity to grab the prize and make off with it[13].

Intrigued by the life-style of the scarab, the creation myths of the early Egyptians regarded the beetle as sacred, in particular the hatching and emergence of the beetle from the ground which they interpreted as 'bringing up a piece of primordial earth (and hence conscious enlightenment) from the watery abyss'[14].

The relationship to ancient Egyptian symbols was rather different to that which we now understand, in that the symbol had an intimate affinity to the concept for which it stood, rather than a distanced relationship[15]. Used as amulets, the magical sense of the scarab was strengthened through the Egyptian name for a dung beetle, *hprr*, 'rising from, come into being itself', close to the word, *hpr*, meaning 'to become, to change'. The word *hprr* later became, *hpri*, the divine name for Khepri, given to the creation God who represented the rising sun. So the name and its spiritual significance were intimately bound together[16]. 'For peoples with a mythical view of the world, the underlying principle was not that of logic but rather of an outlook governed by images'[17].

While it may seem strange to us that a whole spiritual system could ride on the wings of a scarab beetle, the peoples of their time were trying to make sense of their world by drawing on available observations. We have better instruments; we can see further and probe more deeply. If in retrospect we interpret ancient beliefs as primitive, we should at least empathise with their struggle to bring order to the environment in which they found themselves; one that still has the power to astonish us. Dumped in an alternative dimension, how would we set about systematising an environment to which we had no references? What criteria would we use?

'Thus the star-studded firmament became one of the most compelling picture books of mankind. This imaginative world led man towards the divine, to the meaning of existence – and he tried to portray this meaning by use of images.'[18]

Astronomers and philosophers are still at it: who knows how our conceits will be viewed in a few thousand years; that is if our still-primitive world

---

12 National Geographic. *Scarabs*. Available at: www.nationalgeographic.com/animals/invertebrates/group/scarabs/

13 Fabre JH (1949) *The insect World Dodd*. Mead and Co.

14 Ronnberg A (2010) *The Book of Symbols*. Archive for research into archetypal symbolism. Cologne: Taschen.

15 Lurker M (1980) *The Gods and Symbols of Ancient Egypt* (p7). London: Thames and Hudson.

16 Evans EA (1996) *Ancient Egypt the Sacred Scarab*. Knoxville: McClung Museum, University of Tennessee.

17 Lurker M (1980) *The Gods and Symbols of Ancient Egypt* (p7). London: Thames and Hudson.

18 Lurker M (1980) *The Gods and Symbols of Ancient Egypt* (p7). London: Thames and Hudson.

survives our current strategies based on self-interest and has not become subservient to artificial intelligence.

In the Egyptian Middle Kingdom, scarabs were linked to Kephri, God of the rising sun, and later associated with the god-king Ra pushing the sun across the sky. The Egyptian priesthood linked the night time underground passage and daily emergence of the sun with metamorphosis of the scarab from its pupal stage. If the scarab and the sun could be reborn from the earth after death and transformation, could this not also be possible for humans? It has even been suggested that mummification of dead bodies was inspired by scarab metamorphosis with the pupae representing a temporary resting condition prior to rebirth[19].

Although reversing balls of turd backwards may seem an unlikely start, it was this bizarre behaviour that must first have captured human attention and singled out the scarab for further investigation of its habits. Even if only in the symbolic sense, in antiquity this insect became a powerful metaphor for the issue of enlightenment from primordial darkness.

'The balance and essence required for a coming into being as a linking of the finite and the infinite dimensions of the self.'[20]

The Pharaoh Amenhetep was especially devoted to scarabs, erecting many great stone statues to commemorate such events as digging a pleasure lake for his consort Queen Tiy (equivalent to our blue plaques reminding passers-by that the municipal swimming pool was opened by Alderman Thomas Jones). But in the spiritual context the scarabs were linked to a belief system which saw them as crystallisations of the creative god, emerging from the earth.

'So much did the scarab evoke the qualities of immortality, sublimation and transcendence that its dwelling, a subterranean shaft leading to a horizontal passage, may have been imitated in the architecture of the Egyptian tombs.'[21]

Practically speaking, it was thought that after death the mummified human body had to run the gauntlet of the goddess of truth and justice, Maat, in the Hall of Judgement. On its way to the afterlife, Maat weighed the heart (representing the centre for feeling, action and memory) in a huge pair of scales against the weight of an ostrich feather, otherwise tucked into her headdress. Failure to weigh in on the side of truth resulted in the heart of the deceased being devoured by the 'Eater of Hearts' (a ferocious looking lion with the head of a crocodile, sometimes including body parts of a hippopotamus[22]) or alternatively cast into the void – either way barred from the afterlife. It was the job of the attendant mortuary priest to ensure the safe passage of the body through this ordeal. In a blatant attempt to mislead the goddess, scarab amulets (symbols of new life and inscribed with pleas to the heart not to

19 Ratcliffe RC (2006) Scarab Beetles in Human Culture. Lincoln: Nebraska. Papers in Entomology. Museum, University of Nebraska State.

20 Ronnberg A (2010) *The Book of Symbols*. Archive for research into archetypal symbolism. Cologne: Taschen.

21 Ronnberg A (2010) *The Book of Symbols*. Archive for research into archetypal symbolism. Cologne: Taschen.

22 Book of the dead of the Priestess Anhai, XX Dynasty. c1100 BC British Museum

betray its owner) were wrapped into the bandages of the mummy, binding the less than virtuous heart to silence during the weigh-in.

'Do not contradict me with the judges; do not make my name stink to the Gods and appear rotten to the ruler of the next world.'[23]

By the Middle Ages, the spiritual status of the scarab had plummeted from amulet to ward off the activities of the divine, to that of agricultural menace. Grubs munching their way through harvest crops threatening famine, bringing them into serious conflict with the Ecclesiastical Court. In Avignon, representatives of pests such as rats, mice, caterpillars, grasshoppers and chafer larvae were summoned to appear in court.

'The proceedings consist of prayers, exhortations, exorcisms and the use of Holy Water... The judge thrice orders them to leave the area with curses and maledictions and the accused who are then released to warn off their fellow grubs.'

As might have been predicted, such ethnic cleansing had little effect. After three days, the second stage of the trial took place in front of the Bishop or his representative[24] and the plaintiffs were condemned and duly executed (while the judge called down curses on their relatives). In addition, in nearby Switzerland, the larvae were excommunicated and the congregation implored to show its solidarity with the verdict by saying three Our Fathers and three Hail Marys[25].

During the Thirty Years War, Pomerania in northern Germany suffered terribly[26]. A nursery rhyme from the period resurfaced 300 years later at the end of the Second World War when it was sung by Soviet troops advancing through Eastern Germany:

'Cockchafer fly,
Your father is at war,
Your mother is in Pomerania,
Pomerania is burned to the ground,
Cockchafer fly!'[27]

The ladybird, too, like the cockchafer, has left its mark upon the human conscience, not as an agricultural menace but as a pest-devouring ally. Farmers sing to her before they burn their fields, encouraging her to vacate the field before it is lit.

'Ladybird, ladybird, fly away home, your house is on fire, your children have gone. All accept Ann and she hid under the frying pan.'

In an alternative history, the ladybird version emerges from the times when Catholics Recusants, who referred to the Mother of Jesus as 'Our Lady', refused to attend Protestant Services, 'as required by the Act of Uniformity

23 Wilkinson R H. @Reading Egyptian Art London 1992

24 Reitter (1961) *Beetles.* New York: GP Putnam's and Sons.

25 Ratcliffe RC (2006) 'Scarab beetles in Human Culture' University of Nebraska – Lincoln Papers in Entymology. Museum, University of Nebraska State

26 Wikipedia: Cockchafer [online]. Available at: https://en.wikipedia.org/wiki/Cockchafer (accessed November 2018).

27 There is a poignant clip in a documentary called 'Hitler's Henchmen' that shows Goebbel's doomed children lined up in order of height, singing this version.

(1559 & 1662). This law forbade priests to say Mass and forbade communicants to attend it.'

'Consequently, Mass was held secretly in the open fields. Laymen were subject to jail and heavy fines and priests to execution. Many priests were executed by the terrible death of being burnt alive at the stake or, even worse, being hung, drawn and quartered.'[28] Later on, my Catholic husband was to show me parchment deeds held by his family, referring to parts of what is now Port Sunlight, Liverpool, witnessing to the sale of land in order to pay those fines.

As a child, I remember being innocently puzzled as to why the bowdlerized nursery rhyme I learned to sing to an indifferent ladybird as she crawled up a dandelion leaf was the appropriate response to one of the few really attractive insects: pretty, she neither buzzed nor bit. It's clearly the same rhyme as the cockchafer version, but one that has lost its menace, and with it any connection it might have had to context. One way or another I was taking part in an ancient incantation to ward off the evil eye.

Nowadays, it is the voracious appetite of the maybug grubs that brings them into conflict with humans, especially in the swarm years, when for no apparent reason large numbers hatch. Prayers and curses having proved ineffective, a considerable proportion of contemporary research papers on Melolontha focus on their chemical extermination. Banned now, farmers can only lament their crops and groundsmen complain in blogs as their cricket pitches are destroyed by hungry corvids, digging up the grubs to eat.

Nevertheless, esoteric traces of the scarab's magical powers still surface in followers of the Mind, Body, Spirit movement[29]:

'This quest challenges you to be creative in an entirely new and unique expression. As you open to this quest, a chariot will take you on a journey through the galaxies and your energy will spiral upward and you will be connected to a vortex containing infinite and eternal wisdom. The chariot is the scarab and you will spin through the wheels of time and space taking in the majesty of the tapestry of creation.'

This on-screen reflexion is brought down to earth by accompanying cookies for black pudding.

While our reactions to maybugs range from 'Ughh' to 'Aaah', not everybody dislikes scarabs: Australia actually imports them to help clean up manure from cattle farms. Nevertheless, the cane toad story should act as a warning to any groundsman tempted to import an alien species to deal with native pests, since they may have no natural predators to contain their explosive breeding habits. For example, in 1935, just 102 toads were released in order to control the grey-backed cane beetle. The toad learned to eat native scarabs by nestling in cowpats and waiting for the beetles, eating up to 150 in one meal. The downside of this ecological control is that there are now around two million cane toads in

---

28 Ladybug, Ladybug Rhyme [online] Available at: www.rhymes.org.uk/ladybug_ladybug.htm (accessed November 2018).

29 *Scarab Symbolic Meaning* [online]. Available at: www.universeofsymbolism.com/scarab-symbolic-meaning.html (accessed November 2018).

Australia, having an economic impact on the cattle industry through increased risk of disease but with no significant decrease in the beetle population[30].

One of the trials endured by participants in the TV reality show 'I'm a Celebrity… Get me Out of here' is to eat live insects. While Western stomachs may recoil at the idea of crunching insects, scarab grubs do provide much-needed nutrients and are an essential part of the diet in some regions of the world. Perhaps we are just more fussy these days. German students in the 1920s were crunching through sugar coated cockchafers[31]. And a nineteenth century French recipe for Cockchafer soup recommends we 'roast one pound of cockchafers without wings and legs in sizzling butter, then cook them in a chicken soup, add some veal liver and serve'. Sounds tasty, and rather more palatable if you leave out the cockchafers[32].

Swapping insects, milk from the lactating pacific beetle cockroach, Diplotera punctata (which gives birth to live young rather than laying eggs), is stuffed with essential amino acids, fats and sugars and is three times the nutritional value of buffalo milk. The unborn young do not have to go to the trouble of eating, since the milk is already present in their stomach in the form of crystals, which releases protein slowly, as required.

As a remedy for mass starvation, factory farming cockroaches to an industrial scale presents difficulties[33] but there is hope yet. Having sequenced the relevant genes, scientists expect that it will be possible to persuade modified yeast cells to go into mass production[34]. However bizarre it may seem, in the event of nuclear holocaust, insect lactation might be the essential starting point to fill a whole new evolutionary niche, since it appears that insects, especially cockroaches, are more likely to survive a 10 kiloton bomb than any other creature. It rather depends on the yield of the bomb in question – and how near they are to the epicentre of the explosion. Even for cockroaches, at one megaton everything is burned to a crisp.

30 Wikipedia (2018) *Cane Toads in Australia* [online]. Available at: https://en.wikipedia.org/wiki/Cane_toads_in_Australia

31 German newspaper from Fulda.

32 Wikipedia (2018) *Cockchafer* [online]. Available at: https://en.wikipedia.org/wiki/Cockchafer

33 Elison A (2016) 'Cockroach milk could be the next trendy superfood'. *Sunday Times* **30th June**.

34 Krishnan A (2016) *Solving the structure of insect milk proteins* [online]. Department of Biotechnology, Government of India. Available at: www.instem.res.in/content/solving-structure-insect-milk-protein

Chapter 5: Names

In 1735, Carl Linnaeus published a hierarchical system designed to bring order to the natural world. And while the fine-tuning of taxonomical classification introduces more names per plant or animal than there are heirs to the royal throne, strata by strata, cockchafers are now pin-pointed: Kingdom Animalia, Phylum Arthropoda (along with lobsters), Class Insecta, Order Coleoptera (beetles with armoured forewings), Family Scarabaedae and Genus Melolontha. So, just to be quite clear, Maybugs is a cockchafer, and a member of the well-known scarab family. However, for her, since names do not serve to differentiate individuals, this is where it stops.

But when it comes to us humans, we are not just any old maybug: while names serve to separate us and tell us about ourselves, they are more than just labels. Inside and outside, they are the house where we live and they contribute to our self-image. Not only do we want to stand out so as you know who we are but also we need our names to help us know who we ourselves are. Deprived of our names we are depersonalised; we become objects. We feel lost. As part of a process of dehumanisation, concentration camps required their prisoners to respond to a number rather than their name.

And so, since names define our place within the community, we need naming ceremonies. In spite of dwindling church attendances, Christenings linger on, with friends who are no longer believers as Godparents, holding the baby awkwardly in the face of unfamiliar protocol.

Alternatively, unwilling to let go of the need to differentiate ourselves, commerce has stepped in and an equivalent baptismal industry has grown up for the uncertain and the unbelieving, complete with programmes supported by pictures of teddy bears and lists of prices for 'Standard', 'Classic' and 'Bespoke Ceremonies', the latter with a script 'especially tailor-made for you'. Classic and bespoke versions include the cost of a home or location visit to assess health and safety risks[35].

We guard the honour of our names; they are part of us; they carry an affective tag: we establish emotional proximity when we call each other by our names. How we feel about the way they are used is a gauge of intimacy. Revisiting ancient Egypt, a man's name did not only serve to identify him but was also a component part of his very being. To deface the name was to bring harm to the man who bore it[36]. Even today, nicknames can be brutal, and without consent they can lessen our feeling of who we are. They can really hurt.

At the other end of the scale, over-familiarity is intrusive. I find myself resentful when my electricity supplier uses my forename to address me. Who gave you permission to lean over the boundary of my personal space which is

---

35 www.civilceremonies.co.uk

36 Lurker M (1980) *The Gods and Symbols of Ancient Egypt.* Trans. Barbara Cummins. Thames and Hudson

reserved for friends? Far from encouraging me to avail myself of your services, I resent your false intimacy: a twitch of negative affect accompanies my antipathetic response.

But the threshold to such a negative reaction can be set very low if one is on the autistic spectrum.

Josh had a total antipathy to names, especially his own, since they triggered the feeling of invasion of his personal space by a trigger-happy sympathetic nervous system to an extent that physically hurt; even the sound of any name distressed him – and he responded as if he were being attacked. Scouring my brain, I suggested we emailed each other using our initials rather than full names. It was as if a weight had lifted from him.

Listening to Josh's experience, a student with Aspergers tells me that for the first time she understands why, when called to the front of the class and asked to take part in a game that (incidentally) involved calling out the other students' names, she could not. It was not that she did not know their names, nor even that they were on the tip of her tongue, but she was simply unable to articulate them. There was a blank at the stage where her muscles should have been organising and sequencing the sounds. Scolded for her inadequacy, she was told she was rude.

Misjudgement, or perhaps hubris, can lead to serious consequences. It is easy to miscalculate, to give offence, since different people will experience the nuances of affect differently, depending on their emotional lability. Leaders are especially vulnerable. Recently, Wang Cheng-Bi, a Chinese entomologist, made a serious mistake when he dedicated a rare beetle to Premier Xi. The dedication praised, 'Premier Xi's leadership in making the motherland stronger and stronger'. The sting lay in the habits of the particular beetle, Rhyzodiastes Temoana – Wang continued, 'it feeds on mould and can be found in decaying wood'. Wang told *The New York Times* he believed the beetle to be a fitting metaphor for Mr Xi who is fighting corruption. 'It's a metaphor for Xi Jinping – and specifically his controls on corruption (eating rot), which will allow Chinese corruption gradually to disappear'. The story went viral but was quickly airbrushed. Wang had pushed his luck too far.

When we die we leave three-dimensional names behind us, epitaphs chiselled into tombstones and memorials. In time, these strokes and serifs of memory will be weathered and ultimately eroded by the inert looking thallus of lichens swelling and contracting, sliding minute fingers between the rock particles, pushing them apart. Our message to posterity, 'I was here', fades.

I am comfortable with this slow exit, which makes room for new possibilities, new ideas. I don't want the world to stop just because I'm no longer about. With the direction it is pursuing, it is quite capable of pushing itself over the brink without relationship to my demise.

But as memory ages, names become a source of embarrassment rather than endearment, holes to be avoided rather than handles to be grasped. Try as I may, there are times when I can no longer remember the names even of my friends, and worse still, of my family. Reassured by my doctor that loss of this branch of recall does not necessarily mean I am on the slippery path to dementia (names are stored in a different system to general memory), nevertheless it is humiliating to find my tongue stopped in greeting. It is not that I have forgotten the person, their affective flavour may still be vivid; what they are called is not even hovering on the tip of my tongue but buried deep somewhere in the recesses of the past.

At the age of seven I was doubtful when told to jump into the lake to see if I could swim, but I did as I was told. It is no exaggeration to say that the ineptitude of being unable to recall a name is equivalent to the experience of near drowning and watching flattened bubbles of air float upward out of my grasp. The aging brain is mortified, psychologically recreating the sensation of water slipping through my fingers. There is nothing to hang on to. Communication stops while I fumble. It is helpful if one can remember to avoid sentences that include designations, stop-offs and destinations.

The recall of names is so arbitrary. We may be able to remember everything about the individual in question without any vestige of their name and then it arrives suddenly in the middle of the night, floating quietly on the screen of semi-consciousness, even if the spelling is a bit erratic.

In spite of the reassurance of this unexpected night time re-visitation, each time the loss happens, it reminds me of my failing powers, breeds anxiety, in a sense is life-threatening – which bit of me that I take for granted is going to absent itself next time? How long will people tolerate such decline? Or perhaps worse, ask kindly but with an ill-concealed trace of anxiety, if I remember? Is she losing her marbles? My nose is rubbed in mortality. It's not so much death but exclusion from life that is the source of anxiety. And this is one of the instances when it would be easier to trundle through life like Maybugs, presumably untroubled by the imminence of termination. The ability to self-reflect is not always psychologically advantageous, particularly when it comes to possible exclusion from the in-group.

The experience of mental incapacity robs us of who we are. Overhearing conversations in a retirement home, again and again one comes across, 'I was a nurse/teacher/engineer'. Afraid of loss of identity, we hang on to what we have been, a practice that anchors us in the past rather than positioning us in the present. Dementia cuts us off gradually, so we become helpless in the face of the future.

Sudden amnesia is even more violent, amounting to rape of the brain; everything we know as ourselves is taken. Claire has had a brain lesion which has left her 'with a past that is a space you cannot enter and a future that is a space you cannot imagine. Without the past, and more specifically, the capacity to create long-term memories, there is no longer a basis for planning and imagining – amnesiacs live in a permanent present'[37].

---

37 Illingworth S & Bennett J (2015) 'Lesions in the Landscape' Wellcome Trust. 'Lesions in the landscape' is a film which draws together the neurological experience of amnesia with the depopulation of St Kilda.

Chapter 6: How do we look?

At rock bottom, Maybugs and I need to look recognisable and attractive to our own species (especially during the term of maximum fertility) and less so to others (unattractive for dinner). But how about the aesthetics? What do we look like to each other? More subtly, what does our appearance tell each other about the other?

There is something about the appearance of Maybugs, and indeed about all insects, that does trigger strong feelings. They generally go about their business completely indifferent to our presence. They are creepy-crawlies, profligate breeders; where there is one scuttling over the bathroom tiles, there will be a thousand lurking in the cracks, waiting to ambush. It's not just that they may bring germs from dark places on their multiple feet – even though we are the least tidy of creatures, scattering the world with our plastic litter, we feel the need to tidy them up. (This is hard on Maybugs, since although they occasionally swarm, they tend to be solitary.) Nevertheless, reactions range from repulsion to more occasional attraction. The internet has many examples representing the three classical responses adopted by our body's self-defence system in response to fear, whereby our sympathetic nervous system simply spikes and we run away, freeze (the brain shuts down) or we lash out.

'I get hot, sweaty, panicky, cry and scream down the street…'[38] *(Avoidance)*
'Freaked out…'[39] (Shut-down)

and

'They don't like my girlfriend's stilettos…'[40]

(Rather than an aesthetic objection, this blog reads as aggression-with-relish as the blogger turns his partner's heels into weapons).

In 2016, headlines in the *Daily Star* warned the British people that it faced imminent catastrophe: 'BRITS LIVING IN FEAR AS GIANT COCKCHAFER BEETLES SET TO TERRORIZE HOMES THIS SUMMER'[41].

'They're here. The threatened invasion of Britain is underway. The beetles, known as Cockchafers are set to terrorize Brits throughout the summer with their high-pitched screams as they leave a trail of destruction. The inch long creepy-crawlies have been living underground for the last four years. But now, having entered their adult stage, they are expected to make mayhem up and down the country!'

Perhaps the journalist was recalling a bumper year on the continent in 1911

---

38 Youtube Amazon Barn

39 Youtube Connor H

40 Youtube Donald Duck

41 Clarke G (2016) 'Brits living in fear as giant 'Cockchafer' beetles set to terrorise homes THIS SUMMER'. *Daily Star.* **5th June**

when 20 million insects were collected and destroyed in an area of only 18 square kilometres. The stiff upper lip is evidently wobbling. An anxious blogger enquires as to whether a maybug landing on her head wants to lay eggs in her hair – supernits? On the other hand, positive posts talk about 'wonder', 'the beauty of his cute face', and one goes as far as to say, 'this evening I was surrounded by hundreds of these beasties swarming around a tree in a Kentish churchyard. It was spellbinding.'

Either way, when we come across them, we have to take notice of maybugs. They look so bizarre, pursuing ponderous lives regardless of our presence. Nothing I do or say seems to deter them from their course of action. To us, they somehow feel and therefore appear threatening.

Apart from the gender discrimination evidenced by the number of flanges on the antennae, maybugs are pretty uniform creatures. This contrasts with humans and the variety we present to the world. We come in all sorts of colours and shades and shapes, and we drape ourselves with an incredible range of colours, stripes and patterns.

My reflection glimpsed in a passing shop window quickly relieves me of any lurking tendencies towards self-admiration. I am an 'old people crossing' road sign icon, an arthritic silhouette tilted forwards, clutching the hand of a stooping man – except there is no man, only a walking stick.

In school, a young autistic boy is clearly attracted by my walking stick. When I surrender it, he shuffles off down the corridor, leaning on it, bent double. He is a terrific mimic: we all laugh; I'm looking at myself through his eyes, seeing myself as he sees me.

I am back in my own school. This term it has been decided that 'something needs to be done' about our deplorable deportment; we all have to learn to 'stand up straight'. We are issued with personal charts and encouraged to earn 'stars'. Possessor of a long back and short legs, I never move out of the red zone, thereby earning bad marks – and disapproval from my House. I am letting the side down.

Nevertheless, in terms of maintaining posture and equilibrium, I've always preferred the idea of an internal support system to that of external armour, even a hairy-chested version like that of the cockchafer. However, there are times, especially when the sacroiliac joint feels as though it's the target of a high-speed drill, when I should be prepared to trade in flexibility for a scaffold that would ease pressure on this point of weakness, a kind of chitinous corset. Lacking such support, I have to make do with lycra, the contemporary equivalent of lacing oneself in stays. Would I be better off with an exoskeleton?

Kafka's bizarre horror story[42] of Samsa, a young man who wakes one morning to find that he has turned into a beetle, brings home the physical limitations of the exoskeletal condition. At first Samsa does not recognise what has happened. His weak legs paw at the bedclothes as he tries to roll over:

'He lay on his armour-like back. If he lifted his head a little he could see his brown belly, slightly domed and divided by arches into stiff sections.

42 Kafka F *The Metamorphosis* Trans. David Wyllie.

The bedding was hardly able to cover it and seemed ready to slide off at any moment. His many legs, pitifully thin compared with the rest of the size of him, waved about helplessly as he looked.'

Samsa tries to turn on his side. He throws himself to the right. He must have tried a hundred times but always rolls back. Out of his element, he flounders like a beached whale.

Fascinated by Freud, Kafka's refers to 'the Cockchafer dream', 'a dream of liberating independence of the body, which although consciousness is silent, will manage everything efficiently while I rest'[43]. Like the Egyptian myths of origin, which describe the beetle as a symbol of enlightenment emerging from darkness, Kafka's Freudian dream not only metamorphises his Cockchafer from noun to adjective, but transforms it from a symbol of containment to one that 'is simultaneously traumatic and liberating'[44]. I need to reassess my relationship with Maybugs.

Samsa is still trapped under the blankets: if he had metamorphosed as a Click Beetle he would have had the advantage of being able to turn over in bed by snapping a projection on one segment of the spine into an adjacent notch. Such an effort produces a violent click as it bounces the beetle into the air, helping it to right itself (although because the leap launches from the insect's side, rather than from its legs, it has difficulty in orientating the position of its landing[45]. Wrong sort of beetle – and he might still have had problems with the blankets.

On her feet, a more equitable distribution of weight suggests that Maybugs is unlikely to experience back pain. Anti-inflammatories, potions and pills trigger stomach bleeds. Lacking an external corset in order to address such problems, I resort to 'Tiger Balm', an oriental looking ointment in a small gold-topped hexagonal bottle smelling deliciously of eucalyptus – and also (although wary of its powers, since it advertises itself a 'Miracle Machine'), a metal box that delivers an electrical pulse across the affected area. In spite of twice being dropped into the lavatory bowl when I had forgotten it was wedged in the back of my trousers, it still seems to work for an hour or so and is rather more effective than TENS[46] – when I remember to use it.

An additional aid is the handrail in the lift to the first floor of my flats, which is set at the perfect height for back stretches. I can just manage three backward arches between the golden voice, 'Doors closing', on the first floor and 'Doors opening', on the ground. Any more does not leave time to turn, compose myself, and present a respectable face to the world.

Even if my personal structural presentation is now in deficit, since early on in the womb, you and I were always possessors of the same basic design:

---

43 Kafka F 'Wedding Preparations in the Country'

44 Liska V (2009) 'When Kafka says We' Uncommon Communities in German-Jewish Literature Indiana University Press 16.06.11. Gal R and Weighs D 'Jumping Without Using Legs: the Jump of the Click Beetle (Elateridae) is Morphologically Constrained.' *PlosOne*

45 Gal R and Weighs D (2011) 'Jumping Without Using Legs: the Jump of the Click Beetle (Elateridae) is Morphologically Constrained.' http://dx.doi.org/10.137/journal.pone.0020871

46 TENS Transcutaneous Electrical Nerve Stimulation

an inner vertical core surrounded by muscles and flesh. This is not so for Maybugs. When it comes to growth, living inside armour plating obviously has its limitations. To outgrow this, insects have evolved along two different routes. Some, like grasshoppers, simply shed their skin when they grow too large for it. The alternative, which includes the maybug, undergoes a number of radical transformations on the journey to maturity. Hatching from an egg into a soft and totally vulnerable grub, feasting on the dung in which she was laid, metamorphosis proceeds to the pupa where she continues to develop. Only when she is fully armoured can she emerge as an adult, with wings, hard wing cases, functional genitals and a decorative casing. She is now ready to fulfil her biological purpose and engage in the production of the next generation.

Furnished with an adult blueprint and an internal support system, we infant humans do not need to come to a halt while we shed a tegument; we simply enlarge, produce offspring and die. Our overall plan is much the same throughout life. Yet while we may have avoided such a dramatic metamorphosis as insects, we do have a transition period between childhood and adulthood – puberty.

Both in humans and cockchafer, the journey from infant form to sexual maturity is guided by cascading hormones secreted by glands. And, while with all due respect to Samsa, it was always unlikely that during puberty I should metamorphose into a maybug, there is an overall similarity in the hormonal process. Astonishingly, in both humans and insect maturation, there is a common ancestry between the particular hormones which regulate the delicate balance between change and inhibition, one which must have pre-dated the evolutionary separation of humans and insects[47]. Perhaps such a co-incidence should not really come as a surprise since, in terms of biochemistry, the most effective ways of carrying out a particular process must surely be limited.

But in terms of my feelings about insects, it is its outer protective casing that acts as a psychological boundary to allying myself with her. Somehow, while I am comfortable with the idea that we are both alive, I have difficulty with the idea of sharing an affective life-line to Maybugs. Flesh does not meld easily with tegument, cold blood seems an unlikely companion to a warm heart. And 'Hug-a-bug' is beyond the realms of my affective imagination.

---

47 Urena E, Manjon C, Franch-Marro X & Martin D (2014) Transcription factor E93 specifies adult metamorphosis in hemimetabolous and holmetabolous insects. *PNAS* **111** (19) p7024–7029.

Chapter 7: Flight and navigation

Since drag is the enemy of thrust, I am ill-suited to fly: wingless, overweight, underpowered. But when I look at Maybugs, she also seems to be pushing the boundaries of aerodynamic design: resembling an ungainly jumbo jet with engine trouble, she is heavy; no one could call her streamlined. Nevertheless, no matter how hard I flap my arms, she can fly and I cannot. Either I need a pigeon breast, or ancillary power to get off the ground.

Scarabs have two sets of wings. The outer ones (elytra) are hard and protective. Underneath these, a double layered membrane stretches across the fan-shaped skeletal structure and veins of the softer, flight wings. In practice, Scarabs use both sets of wings to beat the air and generate increased lift[48]. They have an ingenious double jointing that has evolved between the wing and chest, which allows the flight wings to stretch, flap and fold back beneath the wing cover.

Early attempts to fly by humans, to emulate birds and bees and beetles, seem to have been largely unsuccessful and often fatal. Take the story of Daedalus and his son Icarus. Daedalus is a developer who falls out with the Cretan king, Minos, over a contract to design and build a labyrinth in which to stable the Minotaur, a ferocious bull to whom the King is looking forward to sacrificing young men and women. In view of their quarrel, Minos is threatening to start oblations with Daedalus and his son Icarus. Fearing for their lives and desperate to escape from the island, Daedalus weaves wings from Osier willow wands, and coats them with wax into which he sticks feathers. He warns Icarus not to head towards the sun. But the boy disregards his father's instruction. He takes off regardless and is lifted into an ecstatic dimension by the ability to fly. Unsurprisingly, the wax melts, feathers fall out and he tumbles into the sea, now known as the Icarian Sea.

Legend has it that Daedalus survived. (Icarus might also have lived if his father had employed a stronger adhesive, such as the superglue used by medieval fetchers to stick feathers to arrows – crushed bluebell bulbs sap mixed with saliva. The recipe I followed recommended boiling the bulbs. It was unsuccessful in the sense that my concoction stuck irrevocably to the bottom of the saucepan. Warning: do not try biting the bluebell bulbs since they are poisonous.

Flying is now mundane; a means to getting from A to B gift-wrapped in inconvenience. Check flight, navigate rush hour to airport, find parking space, queue, check in, wade through tax-free-but-somehow-expensive shopping malls, disembodied instructions, cancellations, find a seat, extortionate cafes,

---

48 Westheim C (2012) Beetle Flight: Flapping Protective wings increase lift. *Science daily*. Available at: www.sciencedaily.com/releases/2012/05/120529073816.htm (accessed January 2019).

wait, bored, wait, boarding queue, double booked... these are the discomforts of civilisation un-envisaged by the caveman as he stood by a river and watched a bird glide effortlessly to more fertile pastures on the far bank.

But it is not just practical considerations that spurred mankind to emulate the eagle; there are the aesthetics of flight experienced by pioneers of flight. My father, Roderic Hill, writes to his wife and my mother, Helen, about the exhilaration of flight and aerobatics:

'...an intoxicating sense of freedom seized and gripped one – the pigmy land lay spread like a glorious table beneath... and then the rush to earth as we glided steep down and you seemed to rush into an abyss, free from the bonds of time and circumstances.'[49]

'...we shot up to five thousand feet to have a look at the clouds. It was gorgeous and I sketched and sometimes [the instructor] switched off the engine so we could talk and I passed him my sketches to look at. The colours were marvellous and we dived through clouds and spun round them on beam ends... and it is a terrific feeling at first, you are petrified and your whole sense of thought and life is stunned as it were and your head feels pressed ever so hard on your shoulders especially in a spiral; this peculiar sensation arises because you have huge centrifugal force acting on your body owing to the speed of the turn.'[50]

During six years' service as Chief Test Pilot at the Royal Aircraft Establishment, Farnborough (FAE), Roderic survived 35 crashes. Without parachutes, most of his contemporaries were not so lucky, perishing in the crumpled remains of aerodynamically improbable prototypes. His advice to pilots about to hit the ground was simple – aim the craft between two tree trunks so that the wings break off, reducing the speed at which the fuselage impacts the ground.

There were no wind tunnels to try out new designs and test pilots needed to come to grips with fear. Roderic and my uncle Geoffrey were famous, perhaps notorious, for having taken up a biplane and exchanging seats, a feat that involved crawling out of their cockpits and swapping over in mid-air, to the astonishment of the ground crew when they landed. If this sounds reckless, these young men were gripped by the imperative to explore the possibilities of flying machines, at that time little more than bits of wood held together by a few tacks and string. Knowing how little they knew, it was their job to explore the possible with reference to the impossible, particularly how to avoid stalling and how to recover from spins.

Aviation was in the Hill family: while still teenagers, Roderic and Geoffrey built a single-seater glider in the garage and flew it off Hampstead Heath. It crashed but was rebuilt. Further test flights were curtailed by the onset of the First World War. One of the highlights of Roderic's life was meeting Wilbur Wright, who with his brother Orville designed and flew the first aeroplane. Geoffrey became an aeronautical engineer, designing the first delta wing aeroplane – the Pterodactyl.

49 Hill P (1962) Letter to his wife Helen in, *To Know the Sky: The Life of Air Chief Marshall Sir Roderic Hill'* William Kimber and Co.

50 Ibid.

Born on the edge of an airfield, planes taking off and landing were my lullaby. (In those days the difference was that we heard aeroplanes; the airspace was filled with their chatter. Nowadays, if we listen from the ground, at most we hear a feint hum; our eyes follow the vapour trails, skywriting melts into the upper atmosphere.)

Wartime childhood: aeroplanes are associated with bombing. We learn to identify enemy aircraft, not just by their silhouettes but by the sound of their engines. The world is divided into 'ours' and 'theirs': 'It's one of ours, no, it's one of theirs' (dive into the ditch). Little boys wheel round the playground with their arms stretched out, screaming a descending 'whe-e-e-iou', incidentally domesticating the terrifying whine made by Stukas as they dive-bomb. Crashes in the night are the gaping hole in tomorrow's terrace.

Setting aside aeroplanes – and while we have abandoned the idea of kites, balloons and ornithopters – there is still a fascination with the ideal of personal flight, the freedom not just to glide but to get bodies airborne and fly without a machine doing it all for us; just us and the air. And even if the latest approximation involves jetpacks, the intrepid are coming closer to realising this ambition. On his first flight, Richard Browning managed to launch himself a meter of the ground and fly in a small circle round a back yard. His latest attempt to fly (as nature never intended) involves climbing into a reinforced turbo suit and attaching two gas-turbine engines to each arm and one to each leg. But a pilot needs to control orientation as well as power. Birds do this by altering the shape of their wings as they fly. Richard has learned to control his movements by altering the positions of his arms. He now wears two of the thrusters on his back, and so far he can manages 12 minutes in the air. But interestingly, in order to maintain flight, Richard has to wear a reinforced rigid flight suit, an exoskeleton. Just like Maybugs'[51].

Having achieved lift-off, flight is directional; it goes somewhere. Navigational skill has evolved from the early instruction given to my Father, 'Follow the railway line to Box Hill and turn left'[52].

While Maybugs' flight resembles that of a jumbo jet with engine trouble (rather than the delicate aerobatics of a flying wing), she cannot just take off and go. Her flight path is dictated by the need to find food, shelter and sex, or to cast round for the largest dung ball and a suitable site for its burial so that her eggs will have an en suite larder.

In the last century children had the habit of tethering captive scarabs with a piece of thread and releasing them so that they flew round and round in a circle. What effect this had on a navigational system which was preset is unthinkable. A somewhat similar but macabre piece of contemporary research blindfolds Scarabs and shows that, in order to orientate themselves, they track the sun, moon, and polarised light. To those of us who live in street-lit urban areas (who have long given up searching night skies for the Milky Way), it will come as a surprise to learn that:

51 Gibbs S (2017) Daedalus suit Britain's Iron Man: inventor takes flight in jet-powered. *The Guardian* **28 April.**

52 Roderic Hill (personal).

'...although their eyes are too weak to distinguish individual constellations, Dung Beetles use the gradient of light provided by the Milky Way, to ensure they keep their balls rolling in a straight line and don't circle back to their competitors in the dung pile.'[53]

Most astonishing of all is the suggestion that when dung beetles dance on their dung balls, they are 'photographing the firmament'[54]. 'Research suggests that during the dance routine (when the scarab climbs on top of his ball and rotates about its vertical axis) they are 'forming an internal representation of the prevailing celestial scene'. They also found that 'the beetles were able to maintain their bearing with respect to the presented cues, only if the cues were visible when the snapshot is taken'[55]. As we shall see, this ability to make an internal map is really important when it comes to deciding not only how far Maybugs is aware of what is going on in her environment, but also to what extent Maybugs is self-aware.

However, mankind has finally tumbled to at least one of the advantages possessed by exoskeletal creatures. Ford Motor Company is equipping its line workers with exoskeletal suits to help with lifting and reaching, particularly those on the production line who are standing beneath the car and reaching up into its chassis[56]. Powered by springs, it assists lift and push. In my mind, I toy with discarding the clumsy reference to 'exoskeleton' in favor of Ford's 'Exosuits', much less of a mouthful, liberating. The current models focus on the torso and shoulders. Imagine a whole powered outfit allowing oneself to bounce around again like a two year old.

Mum, mum, please can I have one?

A lot more going on inside Maybugs' unprepossessing body than I bargained for. I am learning how little I know: there is nothing like dipping into entomology to introduce humility into one's view of the world.

---

53 Dacke M, Baird E, Byrne M, Scholtz CH & Warrant EJ (2013) Dung beetles use Milky Way for orientation. *Current Biology.* DOI:10.1016/j.cub.2012.12.034

54 El Jundi B (2016) When dung beetles dance, they photograph the universe. Lund Vision Group University Science Daily. Available at: https://www.sciencedaily.com/releases/2016/05/160512125422.htm?trendmd-shared=0 (accessed January 2019)

55 El Jundi B, Foster JJ, Khaldy L, Byrne MJ, Dacke M & Baird E A (2016) Snapshot-based mechanism for celestial orientation. *Current Biology* **26** (11) 1456–62.

56 Exoskeletons and Metal Organic frameworks, Chris Smith in Interview with Peter Cowley. *Business Angel and The Invested Investor* **14th August** 2018.

Chapter 8: Interval – alive and kicking

'Hang on a minute.' Tina, who is reading the draft, is raising a serious objection: 'It feels as if I am reading two different books'. In doing so she is confirming the concern mentioned in the introduction – how does one persuade comedy to get into bed with philosophy and science? Less abstract, how can I find myself writing in two totally genuine but completely different voices? Do I really have two people inside my head? Tweedledum and Dee who skirmish with each other but are failing to come up with a resolution? And is the conversation worth having? Perhaps most puzzling of all, who is the fly on the wall, listening to my separated hemispheres battling it out?

The problem arises from an ill-considered attempt to write two books at the same time, literally; one a serious book about autism (the ninth, tenth – I have lost count), and now Maybugs, because I was intrigued by her. Both are converging on what we mean by consciousness and self-awareness, subjects that do not lend themselves to levity. Rather than trying to neutralise one voice or the other I intend to focus attention inwards and take a look at how such a dichotomy arises.

If we were to take off the top of our heads we would find ourselves looking at what appears to be a large putty walnut, a brain deeply divided into two wrinkled halves joined by a thick band of fibres, known as the corpus callosum. Under certain conditions the left and right brain are separated, either by severing the two halves in an effort to reduce severe epilepsy (a technique no longer used), or as a result of a stroke reducing the function of one half of the brain. Again, in some autistic people, the corpus callosum may be damaged or even missing. The question that has fascinated neuroscientists is why we need two brains anyway and whether they act together or whether they specialise. In a brilliant series of investigations, Michael Gazziniga[57] worked with a man named Joe for 40 years. An injury had left Joe with frequent and severe seizures. Following an operation to separate the left and right halves of his brain, Michael worked with Joe trying to unravel the characteristics, dependencies and inter-dependencies of the two halves.

Coming from a different angle, but also focusing on one half of her brain, Jill Bolte-Taylor, a neurologist, tracked the progress of a stroke as her own left brain shut down.

In both studies it emerges that the right and left halves can function almost independently of each other. If the two halves are joined, they are constantly cross-referencing but each has its own specific ways of dealing with sensory input as it arrives. As well as internal stimuli from the body (interoception), both halves receive information from the world outside –

---

57 Gazzaniga M 'Severed Corpus Callosum' YouTube: www.youtube.com/
watch?v=RFgtGIL7vEY

but the right brain gets it first in the form of all-embracing impressions delivered all at once, while the left brain receives it sequentially, picking out details and organising the different inputs into a story of what is going on. Broadly speaking, the left-brain is analytical and the right-brain is affective. Combining Michael's research with Jill's oceanic description of her right brain perception when her left brain cuts out, one is tempted to think of them as Martha (active) and Mary (contemplative), under one roof. The system is reversed in some people.

These collective neural circuits in the left brain may feel like a 'homunculus sitting at a console trying to make sense of the impressions they receive and analyse', and Michael calls this arrangement 'The Interpreter'.

In my left brain, my own personal interpreter is very busy, trying her hardest to boost my morale by coming up with stories that put a positive gloss on events – one that I can tolerate – but thereby throwing a bias against anything less attractive. A highly active intuitive sense is embedded in the affective right brain. Sometimes the interbrain chatter is deafening, especially in the drowsy hours before dawn. Never a dull moment: two voices going at it hammer and tongs. When desperate for sleep, it can feel like a hedgehog with in-growing quills. Please stop.

Trained as a scientist but feeling that this focus on the rational was, while not exactly incomplete, somehow undernourished, a series of tragedies brought me to my knees and I learned to listen to perception, to what I was feeling, to intuition and to insight. Not that it is always correct; one learns to juggle and balance the affective with the analytical. So if my text has two styles and these are failing to present a united front, they represent a ping-pong conversation between the two the different halves of my brain. (As a child I remember sitting on the floor and drawing with both hands at once, a skill that seems to have adult echoes in an ambidextrous brain.)

While such a thesis may clarify the dilemma, it scarcely offers a remedy. There is no help for it but to disentangle the two books, finish the one on the spectrum, then grab Maybugs by the hand and follow her lead into the existential territory of what we know about the world outside and ourselves inside. How far do we share the way of knowing and where do we part company?

That Maybugs and I share being alive is obvious, until my brain starts to wander off down the track of precisely what I mean by 'living'. In addition, we take it for granted that we have to be alive in order to be conscious. However, being alive does not guarantee consciousness. We can be unconscious, asleep (or even in a state where individual neurons take time off and go to sleep while the rest of the brain stays awake).

Back to basics: a healthy tree trunk growing in a hedge is alive but the same piece of wood, kiln-dried, lying in a rack of planks in a timber merchant's yard is dead. And since there is no evidence for a nervous system in plants, the implications are that we can be alive and responsive to changes in our environment without being conscious. So we can rule out plants as being conscious.

However not quite; plants do respond to external stimuli such as sunshine, orientating their leaves so that they receive light to make the sugars that supply their energy needs, although some biologists would argue that this responsiveness goes much further than just an involuntary response. 'A plant can see, smell, feel and mount a defense when under siege and warn its neighbors of trouble on the way. It can even be said to have a memory'[58].

In what sense is this true? Research suggests that what underlies these plants' responses to their environment is not straightforward. Take phototropism – the response of plants to light. Decorating the hedgerow verges, dandelions open in the morning (light) and close at night (dark). An old friend tells me that in order to make good dandelion wine, the heads should be plucked before they are fully open, 'at the stage when they are kissing the sun'. Poetic as this description is, it also suggests an alteration in the chemical properties of the flowers as they open and close (they taste different). 'Plants contain a group of genes that determine not only the response to light and shade, allowing it to photosynthesize most effectively – but also change the way it grows.'[59]

So far so good: but it comes as something of a shock to learn that this same package of plant genes also occurs in animal and human DNA where it is 'important in cell division, the growth of nerve axons and particularly the regulation of circadian rhythm in humans'[60]. Amazingly, our 24-hour human rhythm is regulated by the same group of genes as that which is responsible for opening dandelion flowers and turning the leaves and petals of the plant towards the sun.

Anchored by its roots, unlike humans, the plant cannot respond to light by moving its deckchair in or out of the sunshine: it is stuck where it is. But when I fly to Australia I do have to think about jet-lag, it happens; and just as the plant turns towards sunshine, so, directed by the same gene-pack as plants, I am forced to take to bed and try to sleep off the consequences of shifting daylight hours. And it's the same with some insects. Mutant variations of fruit fly that have lost this group of genes have also lost their ability to respond to light.

Sharing genes with plants and insects introduces a new feeling of solidarity with the living world. In the order of things, my concept of 'us' is forced to expand from 'animal versus vegetable and mineral', to 'animal plus vegetable versus mineral'. This certainly puts a new slant on the idea of the 'Family Tree'.

So far, what we are looking at is a reflex response to internal as well as external triggers, ones that are triggered by a chemical or physical stimulus and do not feed back to a higher point of reference (a brain), for processing. In this case, the plant is alive and responsive but not, as far as we can tell, conscious, which is helpful since defining exactly what we mean by

58 Cook G (2012) 'Do Plants Think? *Scientific American* [online]. Available at: www. scientificamerican.com/article/do-plants-think-daniel-chamovitz/ (accessed January 2019).
59 Ibid.
60 Ibid.

'consciousness' is difficult. Knowing what a quality is not is a starting point, even if in the apophatic tradition. However, 'alive and kicking' implies a vigorous response to environmental insult and, where the kick is well-aimed, thought. There has to be some reference point that has made a decision on what is good for me or bad for me.

Chapter 9: Grey world

So often in life we embark on a project and it is only half way through that we begin to find out what it is about. And here we are: radical surgery, Book One detached, peeled off and accepted by the publisher. Maybugs and I are liberated (I hope) and firmly focused on our journey together, which, as we continue, appears to be defining itself as a query about boundaries. But before going any further, I want to look at what we mean when we talk about our sensory perception of the world.

Vertebrate and invertebrate: in spite of her wings, the most fundamental difference between myself and Maybugs is the evolutionary gulf between animals without backbones and those of us who are supported by an internal stanchion. She has a hard outer casing and I do not. What emerges is more than a simple physical difference: ill-defined boundaries mean that we humans are constantly looking outside ourselves for confirmation of who, what and where we are, since this is how we define ourselves and, at the most basic level, how we survive.

But Maybugs' cladding is not just a physical boundary between the two of us; it has a psychological component, in the form of a reluctance on my part to cultivate intimacy, even if it were possible. Perhaps because I am soft-edged, it is out there, projected on to her hard outer wings, that I define the interface between us, rather than at my fleshly boundary. This is the extended ha-ha where I stop and she begins. I cannot warm to her – and I project my separation on to her, seeing her as unlikable. In order to bring respect to our acquaintance I have to stand back from my instinctive rejection and look at her objectively. How does she perceive the world in which we both live? Do we have the same world picture or, rather more importantly, how does our picture of the world reflect the actuality in which we both live?

From amoebae to elephants, humans and insects – and every other sort of creature – we all have to take in sensory stimuli from the world around us and react to these in order to survive and produce the next generation. For those of us who are equipped with brains, impressions stream in through our sense organs in their millions, impressions that translate into a modality that our brains can recognise and interpret. We translate sensory impressions into plans for action and carry these out.

This sounds a simple process, but it is not. For example, in humans it is not just a case of eyes seeing a coloured picture postcard reproducing the world around us. In practice what we are seeing is not actually there at all. And even though it will make sense to us, Maybugs and I are going to interpret the same picture that we see quite differently.

Starting with what is out there: in his riveting book *The Brain: The story of you*, David Eagleman introduces an idea so strange that it is difficult to take on board.

The world we inhabit is grey: it has no colour. Never mind aesthetics and poetics, beauty is not in the eye of the beholder but in the visual processing system in the brain. Colour is an invention of the brain. What we think we see is in fact a picture our brain paints for us. It is in a sense fictitious, an attempt by the brain to produce a coherent story of the reality of the world outside. Our eyes have to take incoming wavelengths of light and convert them into electric-chemical signals that are sent on to the brain, which paints a technicolour picture out of them[61].

And as light-sensitive creatures, we are not all seeing the same thing. Which particular wavelengths we have evolved to receive depends on which particular kind of creature we are. Unless we have visual or auditory deficits, we see what we need to see in order to survive.

'Each creature (including humans and maybugs), picks up on its own slice of reality. Take the blood-sucking tick, which is blind and deaf. Lying in wait for breakfast in the long grass or bracken for a passing deer or dog or human, it does not even see or hear its prey but relies on temperature and body odour to locate a good meal and incidentally pass on Lyme Disease. No single animal 'is having an experience of objective reality that really exists. Every creature assumes its slice of reality to be the entire objective world'...[62]

So what do we creatures make of this grey, silent world?

The electromagnetic spectrum ranges from gamma rays to radio waves. Outside vision, we are unaware of the cell phone messages and X-rays that pass through us. Light is a minute part of this cornucopia, which includes ultraviolet and infrared. The picture we finally see is partly due to how the eye is constructed but also (apart from whether or not it is working properly) how the brain is wired up to interpret such messages as arrive at its visual processing area. So many things can go wrong, either due to connectivity failures in start-up, or due to subsequent damage.

One of the more irritating outcomes of a small haemorrhage in my left eye is that I spend a lot time chasing the cursor on this text, which plays hide and seek in and out of a few small blank pools, only to reappear (sometimes) when I remember to wriggle the mouse. And occasionally words slip off the page leaving an empty slot. This is physical damage and it affects my sensory organ, the eye, preventing some of the information out there from reaching my brain in order to complete the picture.

Perception or interpretation? Jim is colour blind, unable to sort the red and yellow pieces of a board puzzle: this is thought to be due to the depths of his learning disability. When I make him the same puzzle in black and white, he grins widely, his eyes sparkle and immediately he sets out to differentiate the two colours successfully. In Jim's case, the visual messages he does receive are (in terms of the norm) misinterpreted: possibly he is missing some of the cones in his eye, so he does not pick up the relevant incoming signals, does not see what the rest of us see in the same format. While red and yellow colour

---

61 Eagleman D (2015) *The Brain* (p58) Canongate books.
62 Ibid.

blindness are relatively common, one in 33,000 people only see the world in shades of grey. Curiously, they may be the only ones who are actually seeing the reality of what is present. But since the rest of us live in a world that we perceive as full of colour (and are dependent on our capacity to interpret it for so many aspects of our lives), they are at a disadvantage.

Insect eyes and ours are completely different in structure. Eyeballing the core of a dome-shaped maybug eye, there are 5,475 tightly packed mini-eyes called ommatidia; from the surface each six-sided eye looks like a cell in a honeycomb. The question is, does Maybugs integrate the images from her multiple ommatidia into an entire image, or does she experience a kaleidoscope of multiple images?

Like humans, Maybugs' visual experience is not in the eye itself. Each separate insect eye receives the image and converts it into electrical impulses which are fed to the brain where they are synthesised into one image. However, because she cannot focus easily, when she looks at me her picture lacks detail. I am probably more of a blurred and pixillated shape, something in her way rather than someone with whom to stop off and have a chat. Any idea of intimate communication is a lost cause. Because her eyes are bulgy and stand out from the head, Maybugs does have a wide field of vision so she can spot a threat and evade it by taking off before she gets squashed. (In theory, but she is rather slow to mobilise, preferring to start off with a warm up-orientation routine.)

Some of her ommatidia are sensitive to polarised light[63], particularly that of light from the sky and downwardly directed green light as from a tree canopy. She uses this extra sense in direction finding, especially in the evening flights which take place when the level of light is low and prior to the vital processes of feeding and egg-laying. In addition, her cousins, the scarabs, use this direction finding ability to orientate their turd ball and roll it in a straight line. If they encounter an obstacle, they move along its edge until they find the end and then recommence their journey on the same bearing as before[64]. While just over half of human eyes are marginally capable of detecting polarised light, we are not very good at it and as far as we know we do not use it for any specific purpose.

Like our visual experience, when it comes to picking up sounds, the world is silent, there is no noise out there. The noises we hear with our ears come in as pressure waves due to the compression and expansion of air: our brain turns these signals into our auditory experience. But we don't need ears (as we recognise them) to hear since there are other ways of picking up sound waves. An oyster picks them up through a statocyst; a sac-like organ lined with bristles and containing a ball which rolls around triggering messages to the brain in response to changes in pressure.

---

63 'Polarisation' is the orientation in which light waves are travelling, for example vertically or horizontally.

64 Cardiff J (2016) *Melolontha Melolontha: Common European Cockchafer* [online]. University of Michigan Museum of Zoology. Available at: http://animaldiversity.org/accounts/Melolontha_melolontha/ (accessed January 2019).

Whether or not Maybugs makes use of hearing is debatable. Strauss-Durkheim points out that such uncertainty could lie 'in the absence of an obvious organ of hearing, there being nothing to investigate that looks like a human ear'[65]. But he continues: 'although it is thought the antennae are touch perceptive organs, they could be using sensors in their antennae to hear'.

What is not clear is whether or not Maybugs can make use of her hearing if she does have it: we can only surmise. While her wings make a thrumming sound, there doesn't seem to be any indication that others respond to this.

What really matters to Maybug is how to find food when she is living as a maggot underground. How can she find food she cannot see? But in lieu of vision she does have a very highly developed sense of smell, and this is the sensory lure that guides her through the dark earth – and when she emerges, allows her to find food and a mate. In a world which (according to Eagleman) is in itself odourless, she picks up organic molecules floating through the air and binds these to receptors in her antennae (instead of those in the human nose). It is these signals she sends to her brain, where they are interpreted as different smells. Just as with colour and sound, smell is also an invention of the brain: our brain that lights up the sensory world.

Like the tick, Maybugs can sniff out and move towards volatile compounds. And she is selective. What she really fancies are the gases emitted by damaged oak tree roots. And she is prepared to spend a lot of energy to reach them, pushing her soft body through several meters of soil to the source of her preferred food. Oak leaves are Maybug's favourite, which she will choose in favour of other delicacies. This is about valence, and it makes a lot of difference where she stands on the scale of 'this is good for me' or 'this is bad for me': has she really got a choice, or is she, in survival terms, so programmed that she never notices the presence or absence of an alternative?

Odour is also the lure that pulls in potential partners, not directly but in a rather more subtle way. The adult maybug's favourite foods are beech and oak trees. Not only do oak and beech leaves fulfil their dietary requirements, but as the females munch their way through the leaves, the damaged blades give off an alcoholic smell of eucalyptol and anisol. Male maybugs are attracted by this smell; it helps them locate the dating site[66]. The female enjoys the leaves so much that she may continue to munch away during intercourse, at best an awkward congruence since the male has to lean over backwards in order to achieve his objective.

Bipedalism has its disadvantages and we humans tend to underestimate and undervalue our sense of smell. If only we would get down on our hands and knees, we can follow the trail of chocolate powder across a lawn as well as a dog, if not quite so fast[67]. Our noses are in the wrong place relative to the

65 Strauss-Durkheim MH (1833) On the antennae and the hearing of insects. *The Field Naturalist Vol 1-2* ed. James Rennie.

66 Reinecke A, Ruther J, Tolasch T, Wittko F & Hilker M (2002) Alcoholism in cockchafers. *Naturwissenschaften* **89** (6) pp265–269.

67 Smith B (2018) Ted Talk: The role of smell in consciousness (YouTube) [online]. Available at: https://www.youtube.com/watch?v=V34N9YJAMsY (accessed January 2019).

ground. Nevertheless like Maybugs, my sense of smell is also selective: the smell of freshly baked bread drifts enticingly into the street, while cracks in the local drains are a turn-off. And although pheromones play a significant part in the scent industry, we humans can manage without olfactory information, whereas Maybug's life depends on it. Without her sense of smell she will be unable to find food, either as a grub or as an adult, and will remain a spinster in the short time allowed for breeding.

Chapter 10: On the way

So who are we, Maybugs and me? What are we doing here? (I know the pronoun should be 'I': getting it wrong sends shivers down the spine of the purist. Nevertheless, 'me' or 'I' matters not so much grammatically but in respect of the tone of our relationship. Somehow 'I' feels more insular, a Sunday best pronoun, less welcoming than the cosier and informal 'me').

In the murky past of bones, switching from the use of four limbs to swing round in the trees to bipedalism is a significant change. Until recently it was thought that when the forests shrank and fruit became short, apes came down from the trees and grew long legs to make it easier to get around and search for food. Others argue that apes learned to stand erect wading in shallow waters, looking for food on the shores of African lakes.

Tool use not only developed in humans, but also by chimps in the Congo, who break off branches to the precise thickness and length they need and scoop nectar buried under bark by bees. Rather more surprisingly, Caledonian crows also use twigs to extract insects from bark, poking them until they bite the stick so they can be drawn out of cracks. Bees can even be taught to use strings to release sugary rewards[68]. Precisely when humans started to use tools is debated, since the grooves on bones, previously thought to be the earliest tool marks, are now though to have been caused by crocodile bites.

Significantly, the brain enlarges and alters shape. Our ancestors progress from alarm grunts to speech; a cultural mind emerges as we ask questions and tell stories about ourselves and our heritage. There had to be some agency responsible for lightning and thunder, for storms, for the moon and stars; some reason for the hazards of chance. From The Horny skin images carved from a mammoth tusk, to Pan-gu (the great Chinese dragon who divided Yin from Yang and held up the sky with his forehead), to scarabs in Egypt and to Adam and Eve, we have been – and are still – looking for answers to our predicament. And apart from out there, what is going on inside our heads? What makes us tick?

I met Adam and Eve, my first origin story, in 1939, just before the Second World War was declared. In answer to a question to my mother, 'who was Granny?', she went to her bureau and took out a Xeroxed scroll from a secret compartment. She unrolled it along the dining room table – a Chippendale ten-seater which perished in a fire in the Blitz, along with my pink woolly rabbit – and placing a book on each end to prevent it rolling up again she said, 'This is your family, all the people whose lives are part of yours'. More or less, anyway, since it turned out there were few creative limits to ancestry in the mind of the Victorian genealogist responsible for this document. Working backwards, Indian army and tea planters gave way to farmers and a Duke of Atholl who drowned in the river Tay after mistakenly drinking spirits of ammonia rather than the glass of water by his bed (well documented so far), but this document

---

68 Schiffman R (2018) Buzz off. *New Scientist* **6th June.**

went on to claim the Black Prince, who never got to be King of England, the pharaohs of Egypt and from thence made a clear run back to the first couple, Adam and Eve. Later on, my husband pointed out that the Black Death so reduced the population of England that relatives were largely a matter of sticking a pin into preference.

At this stage I lost interest in granny, and leapfrogging the intermediate generations, focused on Adam and Eve. My mother told me the story, although my version is a little different.

Here is this couple wandering innocently around a garden, helping themselves to anything they need – but forbidden to eat from the Tree of Knowledge (or that of Life, but they were evicted before they got round to this). In the 16th century, the studio of Lucas Cranach produced many different paintings capturing various stages of the Fall, from the last hesitant moment of innocence to seduction. Not only do the postures of Adam and Eve differ but the apples themselves are occasionally born on a tree with fig leaves, although sometimes the artists get round this botanical eccentricity by using entire leaves rather than palmate to disguise the more intimate areas of the body. One of the more tender portraits is that by Lucas Cranach the Younger. It appears to involve three apples. Adam is holding one in his right hand and Eve holds one in each. Inevitably the temptation grows too great and she has already taken her first nibble; the tooth-marks are clearly visible. Retribution is instant: innocence is already lost and leafy twigs conveniently conceal private parts. Adam is scratching his head in a gesture that suggests he is puzzled at this sudden change in their circumstances. Wound on a branch, the serpent hangs over Eve's shoulder, urging her on, 'Go on, you know you like it'. We are familiar with the rest of the story: innocence falls away: knowing good and evil, the first couple are expelled from Paradise.

Brooding on this amazing story, Hebrew scholars added many different addenda. One rabbinical legend suggests that before the Fall, Adam and Eve had 'a kind of horny skin', and that God stripped them of it when they transgressed[69, 70].

Dismissing the joker who is whispering in my ear, 'So that's where the exoskeletal carapace went', I wonder what has prompted this elaboration of the Fall in the distant imagination of the commentator? Which aspect of the story was he trying to highlight? While the legend of the lost horny skin may appear extravagant (even in the context of one of the most powerful stories of our origin), could it relate to an idea in the story-teller's mind that, in order to acquire self-confirmation and knowledge, and establish an out-reach defence system, human beings have had to extend beyond the physical and psychological limitations of their soft boundaries? So in terms of evolution, it would have been advantageous for the brain to expand and develop a powerful cortex. The analogy is attractive and I shall return to it later.

While the location of the Garden of Eden is very specific (a fertile land

---

69 Greenblatt S (2017) *The Rise and Fall of Adam and Eve*. Bodley Head.

70 Ginzberg l (1909) *The Legends of the Jews* Vol 1 p42. Providence University.

hemmed in by four rivers, the Pishon, the Gihon and the more familiar Tigris and Euphrates), the snake first makes his appearance in the Epic of Gilgamesh which precedes the Torah version – and the one which appears in Genesis. The moral dimension of the story stems from St. Augustine, who struggled with his own desire and projected blame for the Fall to Eve. Maybugs is well out of the subsequent misogyny.

However, if we go right back to our beginnings, the murk from which our fishy ancestors emerge also presents us with a loss of innocence, analogous in a remote way to the second Genesis expulsion story[71]. As time passed, some of our simple progenitors specialised, developing cells that were sensitive to light, even if originally it was just that they became aware of shadows crossing light sensitive cells. This sensory sensitivity brought with it an emergent capacity for sight, and with this, knowledge about the surrounding world and its intentions – valence, what is good for us or bad for us (incidentally stripping us of our innocence): a feint biblical echo of biting the apple and, critically, the acquisition of which circumstances facilitated our survival. Increased knowledge and loss of innocence are two sides of the same coin.

To put it brutally, five hundred and fifty million years ago, the Garden of Eden was an unattractive bacterial silt at the bottom of a shallow sea, browsed on by worms with no mouth or gut and strange leaf-shaped soft-bodied creatures: it's difficult to take on board, but you and I emerged from this. So did Maybugs, but she trundled off in a different direction.

With the exhaustion of on-tap, sludgy bacterial food mats, some of the more enterprising worms start to eat each other[72]. This surge in hunter-killers is accompanied by the development of two totally different defensive systems (armour plating and jointed limbs in the case of lobsters and insects, including Maybugs), and an endoskeletal ramrod up the inside in the case of our fish-like vertebrate ancestors, who initially relied on swimming and speed to out-manoeuvre hunters. Light sensitive cells, precursors of primitive eyes, become part of a more sophisticated sensory system. If I can see you, I can more easily capture and make a meal out of you – or escape from your intention to eat me.

Feinberg and Mallatt[73] suggest that making some sense of what is going on in the world outside (extroceptive consciousness) became possible as early as five hundred and sixty to five hundred and twenty million years ago. Now the creature can not only spot a shadow and begin to define it but more importantly, can make a mental image to go with this threat.

Then sometime during the Cambrian explosion something extraordinary happened; the number of our genes (the blueprints for development) doubled, and then quadrupled, opening up a wide range of possibilities for responses to evolutionary pressures. Comparing the brains of monkeys and humans, David Haussler has shown that between three and four million years ago,

---

71 Feinberg TE & Mallatt JM (2016) *The Ancient Origins of Consciousness: How the brain created experience*. MIT Press. (In this and subsequent chapters I shall be borrowing heavily from this fascinating book.)

72 Ibid.

73 Ibid.

a gene known as NOTCH2NL appeared. This gene delays the transformation of undifferentiated stem cells into brain cells, with the result that as they continue to divide, there are more stem cells to turn into brain cells, hence brains three times as large. At the same time the brain becomes more sophisticated as the sensory organs become more complex.

To sum up, as far back as the Cambrian period creatures became aware of what was going on round them and could define which organisms had them in mind for a snack. This awareness of physical environment eventually opened the window to sentience (sensitivity to feelings and affects felt internally). With the basic route to human self-awareness already laid down, consciousness was crawling out of the mud.

Chapter 11: Boundaries

Having eaten of the tree of knowledge, been locked out of Paradise, and knowing what is happening (sort of), what do we mean by consciousness? And, in relation to Maybugs, does this mean I can say I am conscious but Maybugs is not?

In practice, trying to define exactly what we mean by consciousness leads us by the nose into a semantic jungle, since we use the words 'sensation', 'feeling' and 'emotion' interchangeably. Take 'feel', for example, as in 'we feel it if you hit us' (physical pain), but also 'we feel upset if you hit us' (an emotional response). In other words, there is a difference between firstly, the automatic recognition and response to the perception of a stimulus without sending a signal to the brain (reflex reaction), secondly, to thinking about an objective experience as well as reacting to it, and thirdly, an emotional response to that stimulus, and reflecting on how it feels.

We have a physical sense of ourselves, derived partly from stimuli we get from the world outside and partly from our internal feelings and emotional responses. If you stick a pin in me, I am going to recoil instinctively from the source of pain; I don't have to wait for a message to reach my brain and send another one back telling me to move away from you. This is a reflex response. But in addition, your activity is going to colour my perception of you, and I am going to file an image of you in my memory warning me to be wary of you, especially if I see you reaching for a pin-cushion. That is, I have an emotional response as well as a physical response to your perceived hostile activity.

Different sensors in our skin relay different sensations, such as the 'feel' of a surface, whether it is stationary or moving, if it is hot or cold. But there is more to touch than just apprehension of superficial sensations. It combines not only with internal messages and responses of pressure from my tendons and muscles to the brain, but also with inputs from the balance system. These tell me not just what I am doing but also include information about my boundaries, where I stop and where the chair I am sitting on starts, who I am in relation to who I am not. If I'm standing on my toes, I am going to feel pressure on the balls of my feet, in my calves and thighs. When I sit down, I feel pressure on my backside, feet, thighs and back, telling me I am sitting. These conflate with information as to whether the chair is soft or hard and at which angle I'm sitting, whether I am lounging or sitting bolt upright. A torrent of sensations and emotions feeds to the brain asking me if I am comfortable. When I stand up, I get a completely different picture of my posture. In addition, proprioception can be an almost secret sense that records information but does not necessarily alert me to my change in posture unless I trip as I rise. I notice only if I lose my balance and am suddenly presented with a threat. Even then, without thinking, I shall correct a 'whoops' situation with a reflex response.

The degree to which I can process the physical sensation depends at least partly on my emotional state: sometimes I receive a stimulus but get an incorrect reading of how it feels. A very simple experiment throws light on the relationship between this under-sensitivity to physical awareness of self and anxiety...

The TV presenter George McGavin has no balance problems when he is asked to walk along a plank while it rests on the floor[74]. However, asked to walk the same plank suspended six foot up in the air, even though suitably harnessed, he cannot move, although he was perfectly capable of traversing it when it was resting on the ground. He finds himself paralysed by anxiety, which interferes with the messages to his brain telling him what he is doing. Locked into a cycle of distraction, his psychological anxiety messages to the brain are interfering and overriding his proprioceptive and balance messages.

Although George McGavin is not on the autistic spectrum, this experiment does suggest a reason as to why people on the autistic spectrum may appear not to receive enough proprioceptive confirmation, leading them to run around desperately trying to compensate by giving themselves stimuli that have meaning, anything that will confirm what they are doing and where their boundaries are. It is not that they are not getting messages from their bodies, so much as that anxiety, which is a prominent feature of autism, is overriding the capacity of brain to process them.

Failure to process these incoming stimuli can lead to a loss of a sense of boundaries. J describes it as feeling as if his body is going to actively blow itself apart. Alternatively it can lead to the sensation of not knowing where the individual stops and 'other than themselves' begins. Chris is explicit about the effects of such disorientation: 'Sometimes I sort of merge with other people'.

Liz says she feels invaded by others: 'I don't know which is me or not me'. This can be very frightening – 'How can I define myself in relation to what is not myself?' Difficult to imagine, but an autistic person with this problem has great difficulty where there are no obvious walls to define the space they are in. It is quite common to see an autistic child wandering around the perimeter of the playground, touching it all the time.

An imaginative teacher sees one of the children in her class clinging to the fence. She says to him, 'Is touching the fence good?' When he says 'Yes', she asks him if she can do it too. He is delighted, now he has someone close at hand who is helping him define where he is. He now has an answer the brain's question, 'Where am I?'

Some people on the spectrum manage to work out ways of giving themselves artificial boundaries. Richard McGuir uses kinaesthetic anchorage to correct his feeling of non-attachment, physically putting pressure on his body by leaning on a bicycle to tell his body where it is and what it is doing[75, 76].

A young woman wears a loose jacket indoors but needs a tight one to contain her when she is outside. Inside, the walls set limits on the space and she can manage, but outside there are no boundaries and space is limitless. By wearing a tight coat, she maintains the sensation of her body's boundaries.

74 BBC 4 (2017) The Incredible Human Foot. (No longer available.)

75 McGuir R (2014) I Dream in Autism.

76 Caldwell P (2017) Hall of Mirrors: Shards of clarity. Hove: Pavilion Publishing and Media.

And a child who is quiet in his small classroom walks around compulsively beating the boundaries of his play yard with a plastic hoop during break time. He has lost his sense of self in relation to where he is and is giving himself physical feedback about the limits of space. He only stops and relaxes when he spots his image in my camera lens. Now he is able to check visually on his low proprioceptive perception of his image.

Maria sits on the floor all the time where she can feel herself on a secure base. She will not go out at all, hanging on to the door frame and bellowing. She no longer has physical boundaries and is clearly terrified. Using gesture, I point to the door and, still using gesture, point back to the floor where she is sitting, making it quite clear that we are coming back here where she will feel contained and safe. Once she understands, she gets up, takes my hand and comes with me. She is no longer afraid.

The degree to which any of us can organise our mental images varies. In particular, lacking such a protective fence can leave some autistic people feeling extremely vulnerable, with the consequence that they find it difficult to know not only *what* they are but also *who* they are[77]. In order to counter this uncertainty, they give themselves strong physical stimuli that are part of their hard-wired repertoire, instantly recognisable elements of their own body language. They say that when they jump, bang or scratch themselves, they know what they are doing. They are desperately looking for anything that has meaning for them.

Joe jumps incessantly. A psychiatrist tells him that he has to stop: 'When you go through that door, you are never to jump again'. Joe is an obedient child and when he leaves the room, he never jumps again. But he says at the same instant that he loses his sense of self. Joe needs to give himself powerful self-stimulation in order not only to know what he is doing but also to define his sense of what (and who) he is.

Like Joe, Tito also jumps and flaps his hands to get the feeling of his body: 'I need to move constantly to be aware that I am alive and my name is Tito. If I don't do this I feel scattered and anxious'[78].

Sometimes we can provide an artificial boundary. A young man on the autistic spectrum runs round the outside of his house. He rarely comes inside except to eat or sleep. Every now and then he will knock on the sitting room window and if anyone looks up, he will laugh and run away. This is his only real point of contact with other people. I suggest to a student that she sits on a chair in the middle of the room and, when he passes by, knocks loudly on a sheet of transparent polycarbonate. When he sees and hears this, he comes inside, walks all round her, inspecting her, and then bangs on the screen and laughs. The next time we come, as soon as he sees us get out of the car, he comes running in and knocks on the screen. Now he feels safe to connect. Lacking his own personal sense of boundary, this young man feels so physically invaded by other people that he needs an artificial barrier to protect him against what he experiences as physical assault set off by their proximity.

---

77 Joe' story, in a publication by Autscape, now out of print.
78 Tito. 'The Reason that I jump'.

Unlike Maybugs, we humans lack a protective fence, and even those of us not on the autistic spectrum can feel invaded if people with whom we are not intimate encroach on our personal space. If our sense of boundaries is any way compromised, we are going to try to clear a space for ourselves and reach beyond our discomfort. In the search for embodiment we are constantly looking for confirmation of ourselves beyond our personal physical boundaries.

At the opposite end of the scale, Steve, who is not autistic, is a talented young climber. He trains continuously and is completely at home in his body; his stillness is arresting. When he shakes hands, his fingers and palms feel like granite slabs. He does not move unless he needs to do so. Meanwhile he gives me perfect attention. It seems that his constant interaction with rock has given him all the proprioceptive feedback he needs; it is almost as if he has grown external armour plating, but this does not separate him from the world outside. He has a strong physical sense of his own boundaries and, being complete in himself, he does not need to reach outside himself all the time for confirmation. He is already fully self-aware. Steve has what is in effect an exoskeleton. He knows where he starts from and what shape he is.

Sensations not only tell us what we are but they help define who we are. Conversely, loss of physical sense of self impacts on our psychological feeling of who we are, which is rather more elastic than that of our physical self; it can change dramatically when circumstances alter. Take this description by Aziz of the claustrophobic effects of his prolonged incarceration[79]. While he waits to know if he will be allowed to settle in Australia, Aziz is a refugee in detention on Manus Island, Papua New Guinea. At the age of 15 Azis escaped from Sudan when his village was burned down. Now 24, he has done nothing wrong but due to immigration policies there are no time limits set for this limbo-like state. He is scared, 'being in a cage for a long time is affecting the brain'. In a series of phone-calls he says, 'The environment takes control. There is nothing to do. My chest is beating up into my mouth. I cannot eat. I feel like the room is just getting narrower and narrower every day. I'm just trembling.' As Azis' psychological sense of his personal space closes down it impinges upon his physical and psychological awareness of himself. Feeling threatened, he searches for a reason: 'I still feel like my heart is saying to me, "this is your fault, this is your fault". Someone must be to blame.'

It is usual to differentiate between consciousness (as being sensorily aware of one's physical and affective state in relation to the world out there, coupled with a gradually emerging sense of self-awareness), and an accompanying growth in identification of myself as personal entity: 'I am here now, I am aware I am here'. I can also think about being aware that I am aware I am here. And, like mirrors placed opposite each other, with eye-balling images receding into the distance, I can even think about thinking about this: introspection ad infinitum.

---

79 Abdul Aziz Muhamet (2017) In: M Green, A Dao, A Neville, D Affleck & S Merope (Eds) *They Cannot Take the Sky*. Allen and Unwin.

Chapter 12: Brain maze

For the laywoman/man/layperson/me, finding one's way round the brain and learning the names of the different parts is an Everest climbing challenge, partly because of its immense complexity, but also since (mainly for historical reasons) some of its parts have multiple designations. At its simplest, there are three main divisions – the Forebrain, Midbrain and Hindbrain – but these areas do not always correspond to functional systems. In search of enlightenment, I trawl the aisles of Blackwells Bookshop, sifting through pop-up books, dreaming of shoplifting a too expensive ceramic model that opens out to reveal deeper and deeper layers and their spatial relationships to each other. It becomes clear that the current emphasis has shifted from discrete units to interdependence.

What happens to the millions of stimuli that are bombarding us all the time: the sensory data pouring in, the messages running in all directions? Firstly, since the messages are going in different directions, which one is going where? Visualise a London Underground map. Branches from the suburbs plunge into a central loop, which links the main termini. These incoming tracks are known as afferent. Those departing from main line stations for the periphery are called efferent (outgoing). There are numerous stations in between departure and point of arrival. For the innocent, it is easy to get on the wrong train or jump off at the wrong station.

In addition, messages to the brain come from two different sources: one telling us about the state of the world outside (exteroception) and the other about the world inside our bodies (interoception). Two rivers meet. Set this tidal wave of information against a brain that needs to maintain an optimum level of efficiency (homeostasis) in the face of a changing and challenging environment, and you come up against what is known as the 'hard problem'. How do we get a conscious picture of what is happening in terms of pain, temperature, itch, sensual touch, muscular and visceral sensations, vasomotor activity, hunger, thirst and 'air hunger'?[80] How do we turn a two-dimensional sensory experience into the all-embracing three dimensional experience of feeling?

Tap into another memory. I am at school. Miss Guillam, a geography teacher, arrives in class with a wheelbarrow full of clay, a cheese-cutter (a length of wire with a toggle at each end) and a cloth-backed Ordinance Survey map of the locality. 'Right', she says, 'today we are going to start learning about the landscape. Clear the tables.'

It sounds simple – but this is more than just a cartographical exercise about the small-scale hills and valleys of Somerset. As our eight-year-old fingers mould the clay into shape, it opens up the relationship between what we see on the flat map and what is out of the window: we literally learn to feel inside ourselves the difference between two dimensions and three.

---

80 Craig AD (2003) Interoception: the sense of the physiological condition of the body. *Current Opinion in Neurobiology* **13** pp500–505.

When we have completed our models to Miss Guillam's satisfaction, we use the cheese cutter to slice them vertically into profiles – and horizontally into contours. Who wants sat-nav? I have elevations impressed in my fingertips. I can feel those rippled slopes in a way denied to generations reared on rather more accurate laser mapping.

Inside us, neuroscientists are beginning to unravel a picture of a body full of spy cameras, gathering information about sensations and transmitting a rolling 'state of the body' report to the Insula[81]. The insula is the map room of the brain, responsible for monitoring balance (or imbalance) of the physiological condition of the body, a picture that is felt as valence, what is 'good for me' or 'bad for me'. In the insula, the sensation of imbalance is embodied and felt as the experience of emotion. Afferent information translates into feelings (affective state). Now I have a map, I know what my body is doing and have a feeling of what 'myself' is doing.

The insula works hand in glove with the next-door anterior cingulate cortex, which decides how to respond in order to maintain the best possible outcome in terms of energy expenditure. For some autistic people the system does not work out that well: somewhere along the affective pathway there can be a disconnect between perception and interpretation: they may receive a stimulus through the sense organs, feel it as a sensation but not know what it signifies.

In Iris Johansson's fascinating account of her autistic childhood, she talks about this absence of connection between sensation and interpretation. She says she felt hungry, 'but did not understand that this sensation meant she should eat … I was unable to get food if I was hungry and anyway, hunger did not signal to me that food was what I needed.'[82]

Also, 'The peeing business worked only now and then. When the feeling of pee-urge arose, I could feel it in my body but I didn't understand it. It wasn't connected to peeing. Little by little I was able to get the thought in my head that when I had this feeling in my body it was time to pee. It took until I was 11 before I understood that the feeling in my body was pee-urge.'[83]

In addition to failing to interpret physical sensations, Iris was unable to connect with the sensations of emotions:

'Nobody grasped that I had no contact with the emotion field, none that would give me information that other people seemed to have access to. It was not like this field was missing but a bridge was missing, some kind of transfer, some kind of feeling for others. The peculiar thing about my condition is that there is so often emptiness, a standing still, no impulse whatever, and even though I can see everything and understand everything around me, it doesn't give me any impulses for action. It's like being in an invisible glass box.'[84]

Those of us not on the spectrum are inclined to feel that that autistic people do not share our ability to emote – even the word 'autism' reflects this

---

81 Von Boehmer H (1990) Self recognition by the immune system. *European Journal of Biochemistry* **194** 693–698.

82 Johansson I (2012) *A Different Childhood*. Inkwell Productions.

83 Ibid.

84 Ibid.

idea[85]. But many people on the spectrum will tell us that rather than being undersensitive to emotions, they are oversensitive to the feelings launched by their sympathetic nervous system; they are too painful – in order to protect themselves, the brain has learned to bury them.

While it is supposed that autistic people cannot express themselves in metaphor, Izaak, a man with Aspergers syndrome, says:

'If I am feeling sensorily overloaded at college and can't face going to a class, I can only feel it is "bad"; I cannot argue myself out of it by telling myself, "I was really upset at the time and it would have been worse if I had gone in regardless. For me, I can only think of things in terms of absolutes".' He adds, 'I can do binary, 1 or 0, good or bad, nothing in between'. Izaak adds a final explanation as to how it feels: 'Emotions are like algebra, except you aren't given any of the values'[86].

And a young autistic man who finds it hard to interact, buries himself in his computer, extracting excerpts from a tape. 'I'm different from you guys, I'm different from you guys.' He has found a way to tell us how he feels.

Finding ourselves means withdrawing our projections and dumping our introjections so that we can learn to accept and feel comfortable with what we have (our 'who I am quiddity'). This is to embark on a life-work, and one that is at least partially dependent on receiving an accurate sensory picture of the world outside. Because of the different way that their brain is wired and in order to fit in socially, many autistic people at the high-functioning end of the spectrum have to learn to adapt themselves, adopting the ways of the world. They learn that lips curled up at the corners means the smiler is 'happy', without getting a sense of what happiness means in terms of emotion. Building this mask to conceal their autism comes at the cost of a disconnection between how they appear to society and how they actually feel themselves to be, to the point where they no longer trust their feelings as being real. They have built themselves a dried-out exoskeleton, one that never quite fits. The stress between trying to pass themselves off as 'normal'; who they feel themselves to be, frequently becomes overwhelming, ending in a complete nervous breakdown, or, as autistic people call it, 'burn-out'. Instead of denying how a person feels, we need to find ways of validating their negative feelings so that they can feel comfortable with who they are.

---

85 The word 'autism' comes from the Greek word 'autos', which means 'self'. It describes conditions in which a person is removed from social interaction. In other words, he becomes an 'isolated self'. Eugen Bleuler, a Swiss psychiatrist, was the first person to use the term.

86 Izaak. Personal Communication

Chapter 13: So what does Maybugs feel?

The evolution of different species has lurched along through a series of catastrophes which has at times nearly, but not quite, extinguished particular branches of living organisms. Although outwardly physically different, battling to maintain themselves in the face of ecological upheavals, insects and humans have developed in the same world and have had the same problems to solve: birth, growth, eating, mating and self-defence.

Much of the research on feeling emotions in insects (sentience) refers to the maybug's extremely remote cousins, the fruit flies. These minute and irritating flies which crawl all over overripe fruit are extremely easy to breed and therefore cheap subjects for investigation. Leave a banana out to rot and your experimental substrate appears almost instantaneously. Enquiry focuses on their behavioural responses. I can only justify using examples from such a distant cousin of Maybugs, on the grounds that their external skeleton encloses a very small brain. Brain size does not seem to be a limiting factor.

And yet insects, especially fruit flies, are so very, very small, how can they have room for anything we would recognise as a brain? To return to my zoology examination and being unable to label the parts of an insect brain, I find myself in distinguished company since the great taxonomist Linnaeus missed the insect brain altogether[87]: one of his diagnostic criteria for being an Insect was that the they lacked any sort of a centralised brain.

Since insects look robotic, it is tempting to regard them as little more than jointed machines with an embedded control device. My instinctive response to them, which turns out to be quite wrong, is that they are incapable of 'feeling'. They just do not seem to be that sort of thing (object rather than subject). However, the overall picture of insect brains is one of astonishing diversity, with the ability, when necessary, to develop complicated systems to cope with specialised ecological niches. For example, the Honey bee can be taught to count from one to ten, including the figure zero; a concept not embraced and incorporated by humans in their mathematical systems until the third century[88]. But the ability to learn is not necessarily the same as the capacity to feel.

Anthropomorphism is the hurdle. In 1933, Professor Eltringham FRS, author of *The Senses of Insects*, wrote: 'I find it difficult to believe that butterflies, assembled on buddleia flowers, ripe plums or other attractive objects, eagerly extracting their juices, fanning their wings in the sun and waving their sensitive antennae in all directions, are not experiencing

---

87 Linnaeus C *Systema Naturae* (10th Ed).

88 Howard SR, Avargues-Weber A, Garcia JE, Greentree AD & Dyer AG (2018) Numerical ordering of zero in honey bees. *Science* **360** (6393).

something rather more than the mere unconscious adjustment to material appetite… and it is hard not to see in other creatures the celebratory sensations we experience when we see an explosion of butterflies on a buddleia on a sunny day.'[89]

But we do have to try to avoid investing creatures with human feelings – and if insects cannot tell us how and what they feel we can look at their brain structures and see if they have the analogous bits for a particular degree of consciousness. What relevant sense organs and brain parts have insects got that underpin what we know of similar areas in our brains? Can we deduce anything about how these might support their affective capacity: does this relate to their ability to emote (or fail to emote)?

One way of looking at consciousness is to trace its evolution. Where did being aware of and responding to one's environment begin? And what happened when the different branches of the animal kingdom fanned out in different directions?

Feeling sensation and emotion, and the evolution of consciousness, are bound up with each other. And the more we think about what consciousness means and where it originated, the more it becomes clear that we are talking about an assemblage of different states.

Before we can be conscious we have to be aware of our self as an entity, as distinct from a world 'out there', beyond us. We must be able to differentiate our self from what is not our self; 'me' from 'not-me'. We need our boundary. In his fascinating book *The Ancient Origins of Consciousness*, Feinberg summarises the evolution of consciousness as comprising three different levels of awareness[90]. The first level involves the development of sensory organs, which perceive and differentiate the world outside from the self. Fossil evidence shows that eyes developed in fish-like creatures in the Cambrian period, followed by organs for smell, touch and hearing, which enabled these early brains to construct multi-sensory images. This primal level of awareness concerns responses to stimuli from the external environment (exteroception). These are reflex responses to mapped images of the external world as perceived by vision, smell, hearing, taste, sharp pain in the skin and touch receptors. They do not in themselves involve valence – 'add-on' feelings of 'this is good for me', or 'this is bad for me' messages.

Emotions come at the other end of the scale. These involve affective awareness referred to as the 'self'. They assign values to internal and external sensory processes. 'For an animal to be sentient, it must be capable of experiencing its own affective state.' Feinberg goes on to discuss a number of criteria for the acquisition of this level of consciousness, including a variety of distance senses with a high level of resolution (for example, large compound eyes in insects) and the presence of structures with functionally the same form and structure as in the human brain (although not the same structures)[91].

In between comes the capacity to experience both inner body sensations

---

89 Eltringham H DSc FRS (1933) *The Senses of Insects*. Methuen Monograph.

90 Feinberg TE & Mallatt M (2016) *The Ancient Origins of Consciousness* p129. MIT Press, Cambridge Mass. London, England.

91 Ibid.

(interoception) and the external environment, both as local mental images and global inner body/visceral and affective states[92].

So what sort of experience are we referring to when we talk about what Maybugs sees? Combining the different viewpoints received by her ommatidia, her observatory gives her an all-round picture – and an early warning system for detecting peripheral predators. She also has specialised ommatidia to detect polarised light, which helps her to set her internal sat-nav. In this respect Maybugs shares our capacity to achieve consciousness, to know what is happening in the world outside herself, since she can make visual and other sensory maps in the back of her brain, corresponding to what she can see. But she must also be able to merge the sensory inputs from different senses and have localised areas for memory and mechanisms for selective attention. And her reactions to threatening circumstances suggest that she experiences fear.

For humans, our response to fear is dependent on the proximity of the threat: the closer the threat appears, the more brain activity is focused in the instinctive reflex system. The further away it is, the longer time the brain has to consider alternative strategies. So, a tiger on my doorstep, and I bolt: a tiger up the road and I adopt the rather more affective strategy of working out my best option, such as shutting the doors and windows to keep it out of the house. Having a large cortical brain allows me to make a choice: lacking this, presumably Maybugs does not have such an option[93].

In this case, it is difficult to explain the behavior of the male scarab (Maybug's first cousin) as a simple reaction, when he is pushing his dung ball up the steep and slippery side of an unstable sand dune, looking in vain for a damp place to bury his precious food store and serve as a nursery for his young. Every time he nearly reaches the top, the dry sand slides away under his feet and he and the ball slither back down to where they started. He tries again and again. Eventually, after many attempts, the scarab is exhausted. But instead of persisting until he dies of desiccation or exhaustion, he makes a choice, decides to call it a day, climbs on top of the dung ball (it's a good take-off pad) and opens his wing cases, freeing up his rear wings. In spite of the fact that he can have little energy to spare after his titanic struggle with the slippery sand dune, there is no warm-up routine: his comparatively clumsy body just takes off to find a more promising venue[94].

Somewhere in this scarab's brain/body is the recognition that living to fight another day is more likely to conserve his gene-line than struggling on until desiccation and death. He has made a decision with valence, between continuing to attempt the hopeless task of pushing the dung ball up the slippery slope and flying off in search of a better location, which is rather more sophisticated than just an automatic reflex. How did he know which strategy to choose if he could not recall his previous attempt and reflect on the

92 Ibid.

93 Mobbs D, Petrovic P, Marchant JL, Hassabis D, Weiskopf N, Seymour B, Dolan RJ & Frith CD (2007) When fear is near. Threat imminence elicits prefrontal-periaqueductal gray shifts in humans. *Science* **317** (5841) 1079–1983.

94 Sahara (2018) BBC 4. **4 July**. (David Attenborough refers to the scarab as 'she', although it is normally assumed that the pusher is male.)

hopelessness of continuing the struggle? How could this have happened unless there were images and internal maps and memory to assist comparison?

Further abroad in the insect world, Matabele ants also behave as if their brains can make mental maps that enable them to compare two different scenarios. These ants live in small colonies so they cannot afford to lose defensive members. During their frequent battles with termites, they rescue warrior ants who have lost a limb and lick their wounds. Piggybacking them to the nest, they continue to nurse them. Of those that receive this treatment, 90% survive. Of untreated ants, 80% die. (It is supposed that the saliva may contain an antibiotic to resist infection.) But the rescuers are also selective, choosing the less badly injured (one leg missing and still able to hobble to war) and ignoring the soldiers who have lost five legs, so will clearly be no further use as warriors[95]. While this does not necessarily infer that these ants can count, it does suggest that their brains have developed the ability to assess and compare one state with another, to do which they would have had to evolve the capacity to make a mental map. (This apparently nurturing behaviour also raises the question of how much of my engagement with others is self-centred and how much of it springs from a genuine shift of self-interest to altruism and empathy? And where does my interest in what lies beyond advantage to my immediate self begin?)[96].

While it is already clear that my seemingly robotic Maybugs is likely to be a lot more aware of her surroundings than I had given her credit for, I want to know just how far this sensitivity goes. The question is simple, do insects – any insects – 'feel' their fear?

When fruit flies are confined in a Petri dish, they abandon the open space in the centre and fly away from a shadow that mimics a predator, heading for the relative shelter of its walls. This behavior increases the more often the threat is presented, not just at the time of presentation but for minutes after the threat is withdrawn. Helen Whiteley[97] points out that if they are given a dose of valium, or if the mushroom bodies (the parts of the insect brain equivalent to the human limbic system) are removed, the flies are no longer anxious and do not seek the walls. This suggests that fruit flies do have a mental image necessary to underpin an emotional feeling, at least of fear.

So much for response to fear; how about the imperative for sex? In the absence of female fruit flies, males will attack each other, a level of aggression that rises in the presence of sex pheromones. And they drink more alcohol (ethanol) when derived of female company. While it is tempting to see in this latter response a rejected lounge lizard propping up the bar, an alternative explanation is that, rather than a purposefully drowning their sorrows, too

---

95 Fox-Skelley J (2017) Ants care for wounded comrades by licking their wounds clean. *New Scientist*. **14 February.**

96 Ibid. (p185).

97 Comment by Whiteley H, research assistant, Neuroanatomy Strasbourg, France, on Anderson D (2016) 'Do Fruit Flies Have Emotions?' An interview with David Anderson at TEDxCaltech.

much to drink is simply a continuation of the search for reward[98]. Nevertheless, in what sense are these responses indicative of 'feeling' anxiety, anger and fear?[99] Perhaps it is just due to my preconceptions of what is or is not likely, but somehow the image of a love-sick fruit fly is completely ridiculous. While Maybugs reacts to sensory awareness indicative of 'time for a feed', 'time for coition', it seems doubtful whether we can call these sensations 'emotions'. Or are they?

Looking at bumblebees… bees that are given a reward of sucrose syrup behave more adventurously when foraging. They are also braver if they think they are being attacked than those who have not received a sugar treat. This is not due to a sugar-high but related to a dopamine hit, suggesting what would be interpreted in humans as an emotional response[100]. This calls into question what we ourselves mean when we say we have 'emotional responses'; we 'feel happy': one begins to agree with Henry Marsh[101] when he is discussing dualism and our deeply seated belief in mind and body as separate entities: 'My "I", my conscious self, does not feel like electrochemistry, but that is what it is'.

The arguments swing back and forth. The neuroanatomist Budd Craig[102] has recently identified a system for carrying sentient messages, but only in primates and humans – and one that is missing in insects. On the other hand, Bjorn Merker says that insects do have a midbrain part of the brain and this could support consciousness[103]. The question is which bit of consciousness – visceral awareness or the ability to reflect on the experience leading to self- awareness.

In addition to hard-wired behaviour, and in spite of their tiny brains, insects can memorise and learn, some better than others. But the capacity to learn, even such complex abstract ideas as zero, is not the same as an affective response.

Looking inside scarabs, it appears they are well supplied with brains, they just look different. The main brain (forebrain), rides above the gullet, looping down round it to another below. (To call the latter less important may possibly mean that its function has not yet been fully explored.) In addition, as in earlier stages of evolution when the arrangement of the body was clearly segmental, each segment of her body also has its own collection of nerve cells (ganglion). Those scarabs which feed on a general diet rather than just dung have developed complex 'mushroom bodies', with folds like a vertebrate brain, which are the seat of memory and learning – and lead to sophisticated behaviour

98 Shohat-Ophir G, Kaun K R, Azanchi R & Heberkein U (2012) Sexual deprivation increases ethanol intake in Drosophila. *Science* **335** (6074) 1351 DOI: 10.1126/science.1215932

99 Comment by Whiteley H, research assistant, Neuroanatomy Strasbourg, France, on Anderson D (2016) 'Do Fruit Flies Have Emotions?' An interview with David Anderson at TEDxCaltech.

100 Perry CJ, Baciadonna L & Chittka L (2016) Unexpected rewards induce dopamine-dependent positive emotion-like state changes in bumblebees. *Science* **353** (6307) 1529–1531.

101 Marsh H (2017) *Admissions: A life in brain surgery*. London: Weidenfeld & Nicholson.

102 Craig B (2014) 'How do you feel?

103 Klein C, Barron A. (19.04.16)' What insects can tell us about the origins of consciousness. - NCBI Proc Natl Acad Sci U S A. 2016 May 3;113(18):4900-8.

patterns[104]. Interference with their development leads to short and long-term memory loss.

Given the incredible structural diversity of insects and arthropods in general and insects in particular, here is Feinberg's big question. Why have I, Everyman, Everywoman, Human Being, Whoever, inherited a big brain that is self-aware (the part that lets me say 'I am') while, although she can feel, Maybugs does not seem to have the bits of the brain which initiate and sustain self-awareness? (At least, no-one has found them yet.) Why did she never manage to evolve a large forebrain, which would have allowed her to feel, in the sense of being able to reflect on her emotions and having a sense of self-hood?

It does seem to me that there are two questions here. One is about ecological pressure. What was it that the human brain was responding to that favoured big brains. A recent paper in *Nature* uses a computer model to show that environment had a stronger influence than social challenges: 'About 60% of the increase in brain size over our ape ancestors came as a result of surviving in the environment, finding and caching food, 30% from banding together to survive and the remaining 10% from competing with other groups.'[105] (Importantly they add, 'co-operation decreases brain size because you rely on the brains of other individuals and you do not need to invest in such a large and expensive brain'). This is interesting because in relatively recent times our brains have started to shrink 'possibly because we increasingly store and process information online so can probably get by with smaller brains'.[106]

To go back to insects, the second question here is architectural. Feinberg suggests the exoskeleton is a limiting factor in that, in order to grow, an insect has to undergo a stage in its life cycle when it lacks adequate protection: a big soft grub with a large brain would have been extremely vulnerable to predation.

Tentatively, I should like to suggest an additional possibility. As we have already seen, my human physical limits are less well defined than that of my friend, the small-brained/strong-boundaried Maybugs. If I had an ever-present hard boundary I should be getting on-tap feedback – and should not constantly have to reach outside myself for confirmation. So perhaps it was advantageous in evolutionary terms for my human soft-skinned ancestors to develop larger brains, in the search for confirmation and knowing what they were doing in relation to the world. Maybe this is where curiosity came from?

Rather than trying to define consciousness as an unfolding continuum, it may be more helpful to look at the particular way it arises in conjunction with any given situation; as the emergence of different adaptations in response to separate ecological niches and pressures.

Considering what I have learned from Maybugs, I find myself asking how

104 Farris SM (2008) Structural, functional and developmental convergence of the insect mushroom bodies with higher brain centers of vertebrates. *Brain Behaviour and Evolution* **72** (1) 1–15.

105 Gonzales-Forero M & Gardner A (2018) Inference of ecological and social drivers of human brain-size evolution. *Nature* **557** (7706) 554–557.

106 Stringer C (2019) *Why Have Our Brains Started to Shrink?* [online]. Available at: https://www.scientificamerican.com/article/why-have-our-brains-started-to-shrink/ (accessed January 2019).

much of my response to the world is, like Maybugs', driven by valence: what is good for me, or what is bad for me? Are the choices I think my 'self' is making simply more sophisticated versions of those made by scarabs, developed since I live with more variables?

Chapter 14: English lesson

If Maybugs appears to be taking a back seat in this chapter, it is not because we have parted company. Instead she has become the source of my ideas; I am looking out through the visor of her mindset.

One way and another, what we humans know about ourselves is related to consciousness. Those of us who incline to introspection spend an awful lot of time reflecting on who and what we are, and we don't always get it right. In making a distinction between consciousness in general (knowing what is going on), and a gradually emerging sense of self-awareness, of personal entity ('I am here now, I am aware I am here'), I have to start with me, because I know me best – but at the same time I hope to be a stand-in for Everyperson.

At least, I think I know about me: that is, I am ME, both in the sense of a physical entity with boundaries (what I am), and also in the psychological sense (who I am, and, as importantly, who I am not). I define myself in terms of how I feel I am; I have a certain flavour, a flavour that tastes different from all you 'not-mes' out there. And since I am the only me I have, I am prepared to defend myself, with my life if necessary.

An extreme point of view (so extreme that it feels difficult to take on board) is that my feeling of 'self' may be an illusion: that human consciousness is a con trick played by the brain, which builds itself an internal self-model, 'one which keeps track of whatever is being controlled, allows for predictions and planning' and then looks at it[107].

Anul Seth goes as far as calling our consciousness a 'hallucination'[108] (in the sense that one experiences something that is not really there). He describes the brain experiencing the outer world as a prediction machine and the conscious self as, 'the lead figure in our personal 3D inner movie'. Echoing David Eagleman, he says:

'There is no light inside the skull or sounds, all we have to go on are streams of electrical impulses which are indirectly related to things in the world. So, perception is a process informed by guesswork in which the brain combines these sensory signals with its prior expectations or beliefs about the way the world is, to form its 'best guess' of what caused the signals.'

Seth continues that our inner experience of our bodies (interoception) is about control and regulation and is rooted in our drive to keep ourselves alive. 'Our human consciousness generally is just a tiny region in a vast space of possible consciousnesses. Our individual self and worlds are unique to each of us – but they are all grounded in biological mechanisms shared with many other living creatures.' While this view, for which there is increasing evidence, presents no problems to the atheist, it does gnaw at the foundations of much religious observance. The implications are that 'I am', 'Me', is a physical sensory experience of the workings of the body I inhabit. What happened to my soul?

---

107 Graziano M (2016) *Consciousness: The mind messing with the mind*. The Atlantic.

108 Anul Seth (2017) TED TALK *Your brain hallucinates your conscious reality* [online]. Available at: https://www.youtube.com/watch?v=lyu7v7nWzfo (accessed January 2019).

Back to school: my wooden desk (as seen polished up in antique shops nowadays) has a lid that slams down on a tatty pile of exercise books, a groove along the top for my relief pen and a hole for its china inkpot, filled daily by the ink monitor. I am not tidy and much of the ink ends up on my fingers. Our teacher is Miss Parsons. Tall and thin, her hair is permanently waved into curls. We are fond of her. Her bifocal smile peers, is directed towards us but stems reciprocally from an inner glow. She calls us to attention. 'Today we come to the most important verb in the English Language, the verb 'to Be'. We sit up and listen. 'I am' sounds interesting, but before we have time to consider the implications of Being, the quidity of self is swept away in a wave of phonically unrelated sounds. How do, 'u' and 'is' relate to the primary proposition?

The mind diverts: 'I am', is in here – and when Moses enquires of God, 'whom should he say sent him?', the answer is equally baffling, 'I am who I am', and, 'tell them, "I am has sent you"'[109], requiring us to reshuffle any idea we might have had of a relationship to an exterior God out there. But to be a small part of Being is not uncomfortable. Even if the system is divine, it has to operate through flesh. 'Our individual self and worlds are unique to each of us but they are all grounded in biological mechanisms shared with many other living creatures'[110]. I like the idea of relationship.

Anul Seth continues, 'We are growing a sense of wonder and greater realisation that we are part of and not apart from the rest of nature'[111]. Or as Gandhi pointed out, 'a drop of water on its own evaporates in the sun; in the sea it participates in the glories of the ocean'. It all depends what we mean when we talk about God. I find myself walking along the shores of Neo Platonism[112].

Here is the first premise: if Maybugs and I have separate identities, we are still part of this living stream of consciousness. In this sense, we are not alone. Even if my sense of self is an illusion, I am going to enjoy it, since it is a good working hypothesis and a limited opportunity. In order to do this, I am going to have to learn to reach out and confirm my relatedness to other than myself.

So, back to the womb: the first inklings we have of ourselves as a body (even an illusory body can be warm and comfortable), and a world beyond ourselves, is when we sense and tune into the rhythmic beat of our mother's heart through pressure waves in the amniotic fluid. This physical contact starts weeks before our hearing comes on-line – wrapped in our mother's uterus, we feel the thumps before we hear the diastolic beat. Pressure and rhythm come first.

After our hazardous passage through the birth canal, we arrive in this world already primed for interaction. We have to try to make sense of the bombardment of bright lights and noises, so we latch on to anything that is recognisable to our immature perception. Fortunately, just as we knew our mother's heartbeat in

---

109 Exodus 3:14.

110 Anul Seth (2017) TED TALK *Your brain hallucinates your conscious reality* [online]. Available at: https://www.youtube.com/watch?v=lyu7v7nWzfo (accessed January 2019).

111 Ibid.

112 Neo Platonism is a philosophical system combining Platonism with mysticism and Judeo-Christian ideas and positing one source for all existence, developed by Plotinus and his followers in the 3rd century AD.

the womb, she is also primed for interaction: on the lookout for her newborn's initiatives, and if all is going well, ready to welcome us into a world of meaning.

Mother (or mother figure) and baby get drawn into a dyadic conversation, where both respond to each other. This is where communication begins. As Zeedyk remarked[113], both Mother and baby are so absorbed that the outsider feels witness to an interaction from which they are separated, as if they were seeing an interaction going on inside a glass bottle. The baby responds tentatively at first and then with increasing confidence as it learns that, if it makes certain movements, it will get a specific response. So the infant brain uses its senses to probe the world, looking for recognisable answers to its initiatives (recognisable in the sense that they match up to their own movements and sounds and rhythms, to the blueprints they already possess). These do not have to be exact copies but they do have to be near enough and meaningful for the underlying sound, movement or rhythm to be recognised and to match to a template that the infant already has. And if the mother is not to hand, when we perceive a stimulus we normally try and confirm it in a different mode. We become explorers, seeking confirmation. Have I got this right?

It had been thought until recently that the baby was just imitating its mother's initiatives: recent studies suggest that the baby's response to the mother's initiatives may be that of arousal to anything interesting[114], rather than the baby specifically copying. Like a twig sprouting from an existing branch, the baby is likely to take on board a new stimulus if (at least in part) it matches up to a substrate that already exists. Each time we confirm a pattern of which they already have an outline, we help the infant to embody an image of themselves, who they are. Fundamental to this process is the plasticity of the brain. The infant does not just absorb new stimuli – the brain can also rewire itself, forming new connections in response to repeated activities and experiences.

We observers have a habit of looking at things from our own point of view. In this case we are fascinated by the baby's capacity to imitate, the outward sign of an inward process. But what may be more important from the point of view of development is her emerging capacity to make sense of the environment into which she has been precipitated – and learning to co-ordinate the experience of her different sense.

As we confirm them, the infant nerve pathways are being reinforced. She knows that this bit of her brain is working so she can move on to try something else. When the Mother answers the baby's initiative, the infant breaks into chuckles. This is when she recognises her own movements and expressions. So if you, baby, make a sound or wave your hand, I, mother, am going to gurgle or wave back to you. This tells your brain that a particular set of muscular movements/sounds you made trigger this particular outcome in something other than yourself (mother in this case). A pathway of connections between nerves (synapses) is being established in the brain, a step towards

113 Zeedyk S. Comment during a seminar.

114 Jones s (2009) The development of imitation in infancy. *Philosphical Transactions of the Royal Society* **364** (1528) 2325–2335.

'I know what I'm doing'. Mother and baby have established a way of talking that makes sense to both. The mother is confirming what the baby is doing and the baby is recognising its initiatives in the mirror of its mother's response. This reciprocal game allows the infant to build up a picture, not only of its mother, but also helps her infant brain to map her own body. In this sense the interaction is literally embodied.

Damasio explains:[115] if we hear, see or feel an object or an activity, we get two messages back to our brain. We not only perceive what is going on outside but we also learn that our eyes, ears and sense of touch and pressure are in working order. In other words, we are dependent on the confirmation we get from the world outside, for the embodiment of our sense of self. While we are building up a picture of mother, we are also confirming our bodies – the image of what we ourselves are doing as well as what we are doing in relation to our environment. It is this brain mapmaking that allows us to take off in a new direction.

From infancy, our newly discovered senses work in partnership. If we are in any doubt, we confirm the perception of one sense by checking it with another. If visual perception does not give us enough information, we may reach out and touch the surface to complete the picture.

Abi is ten months old. A series of three selfies taken in rapid succession on an iPhone by her grandmother, illustrate the complex part that confirmation can play in physically positioning ourselves in relation to someone else. Abi is sitting on her grandmother's knee, facing outwards away from her, looking at and focusing on the image of her grandmother (not herself) on screen. She looks puzzled. What seems to be going through her mind is the misfit between her visual perception of her granny reflected in the camera lens, and the physical comfort of her grandmother's lap on which she is sitting. In the second photo, she is still watching her granny on camera. Without turning round, she has lifted her left arm and is reaching back to squeeze her granny's cheek (hard), using pressure to confirm where granny is, in relation to herself. It is only in the third photograph that she turns back to look at her granny's face. Damasio is correct. Abi has sorted the discrepancy, using her eyes and proprioceptive sense in conjunction with each other. In addition to her grandmother's whereabouts and her sense of self, Abi has confirmed where she is in relation to where she is not. And interestingly, although preverbal, she is making a logical deduction.

The balance between needing others and protecting our personal space is precarious. Solitaries are rare: most historical hermits seem to have had servants to provide for their essentials. We need each other, not only to service our physical needs but also to confirm our embodied existence. Without the possibility of emotional interaction we are disempowered, cut off from the world we inhabit, not only by physical need but also isolated in a self-spun cocoon of affective sterility.

Nevertheless, it requires a conscious effort to move out of our instinctive 'me first' survival mode, to a sense of other people having equally important selves.

---

115 Damasio

Somewhere along the process of growing up our personal boundary needs to become porous so we can see beyond the limits of our personal experience. In order to engage with them, as well as just to use them, we need to know how they feel – at its most basic level, do we trust them? What does their body language tell us about their affective state.

Aged 14 and tongue-tied at a party, I am standing by the wall and my mother is unsympathetic; her instructions are succinct, 'You must be interested in other people and think about what interests them'. This brutal but necessary onslaught on adolescent self-interest requires a major shift in my personal centre of gravity. Other people have their own points of view? And it's different from mine? Like the Frenchman who said that it would have been much better if Elizabeth I had married Philip of Spain. I need to turn my map round. I have to learn to interact with a world that is using different cartographical projections. I needed to learn to play with ideas, other people's as well as my own.

While we monitor each other's posture relative to ourselves, it is not only position that is relevant. The key to engagement is learning to engage with other people's body language and facial expressions, to listen with all our senses. So here I am, launched on the pathway to finding myself as a person rather than just as a sensory dartboard. But in searching for this thing I call myself, it is easy to look for validation in the wrong place.

We are constantly looking for confirmation in order that we can move on; otherwise we are trapped in a repetitive loop with no outcome. And there is a sense in which we are all (more or less) narcissistic, pushing the boundaries, looking for our own selves through personal and external confirmation, a process that involves both recognition (of an image or sound) and embodiment into physically knowing one's self and boundaries. Recognition on its own without embodiment can lead to narcissism, a fruitless quest, searching for that idealised state where our every initiative is embraced and confirmed without question.

Like many myths, the Narcissus story derives from alternative corners of the celestial psyche, where quarrelsome Gods run rampant, milking the universe to assuage their ennui with eternity. Ovid's myth was almost certainly drawing on earlier texts. From heavily edited versions for children, to a feminist slant on Freud's Narcissus, peering into a pool in the hope of glimpsing his Mother's genitalia[116], it is a myth that has cherry-picked the orchards of the unconscious in search of a particular point of view.

A child of rape, the beautiful Narcissus has a bad start in life. With an absent father, his failure to make relationships with either boys or girls suggests that he may have Attachment Disorder. Or possibly he is autistic , since the poet Ted

---

116 Segal N. 'Narcissus and Echo: Feminine haunting Masculine' 'Echoes of Narcissus' (2000) ed. Lieve Spaas Polygons Cultural Diversities and Intersections Vol 2 p.140

Hughes[117] (with a suggestion that he lacks emotional warmth[118]), imagines there is something 'glassy' about his beauty; one can admire him as an object rather than relate to him: 'none dared to be familiar with him, let alone touch him'.

However, Narcissus' mother, Liriope, is clearly worried about his development and seeks advice from the neighbourhood Child Guidance Clinic. The Consultant, Tiresius, is blind, and his prognosis is equivocal, one that nudges enough of a double negative as to cast doubt on its precise meaning: 'if he but fails to recognise himself, a long life may he have under the sun'. It's the 'but' that is the problem.

Meanwhile, at the mercy of vengeful gods, Echo, his would-be girlfriend, is stricken with echolalia and never stands a chance, since she can only repeat the tail end of his sentences. When she stumbles upon Narcissus out in the woods hunting deer, due to her speech impediment, there is an absurd series of misunderstandings and he rejects her utterly. Finding a pool he bends down to drink and catches sight of his reflexion. At first he does not recognise himself and falls in love with its beauty; 'he loves an imagined body that contains no substance'. He tries to embrace and kiss his image but as he clasps it, it fragments and slips away through his fingers. When he realises that he is split, 'that he loves not a beautiful face in the spring but this double that has suddenly sprung from him, he wants to see himself as a whole, rather than in the form of a floating reflection, which still fascinates him but which he wants to see embodied in his own body'. Realising his love is unattainable, he languishes, 'as did the hoar-frost melt in the morning 'neath the genial sun, so did he pine away'. Some versions allege that in Hades he is still trying to catch up with his lost self, reflected in the River Styx[119].

What is it that Narcissus is seeking that is missing in his self-knowledge when he looks into the pool? What is he actually looking for that he has not already got? And since this is not a true story, why is it so compulsive?

We are given clues; told that Narcissus' hunt for the deer is in reality a search for himself[120] but, as already pointed out, Tiresius' prophecy is ambiguous, an unanswered question. Does the seer mean 'self' in the sense of external image (as in the pool), or, in the sense of quiddity, the inner essence; the 'who' of whom we feel ourselves to be? (Till, my joker, is at it again, pulling my ear-lobe to attract attention, 'maybe he's dropped his iPhone in the water? Or there's a poor internet connection, so he can't even self-confirm?)

Narcissus is confused. At first he is deceived; even though the illusion imitates his movements and leans towards him, responding to his attempts to embrace it, it unravels as his tears distort the image or as he touches it.

---

117 Ted Hughes. (1999) Tales from Ovid Echo and Narcissus, Faber and Faber

118 As an important aside, while people with autism may present with a detached look, it does not necessarily mean that they lack emotional warmth. It may be that they are overly sensitive to feeling and are in retreat from the overwhelming surge of hormonal activity generated by their sympathetic nervous system as a response to any form of emotional warmth – expressed as feeling like being drowned in tsunami of pain.

119 Ovid's Metamorphoses Book 3. *The story of Echo and Narcissus*. Translation by Mary M Innes Penguin 1955. Cited in 'Narcissus reflected' David Lomas p.15

120 Andreoli M. 'Narcissus and his Double' in *Echoes of Narcissus*. Ed. Lieve Spaas. p.16

Imitation re-enforces the illusion. He realises he is never going to find his inner self in this insubstantial appearance.

Tiresius' warning is timely; once the young man realises that this image will never lead him to the knowledge of his true self he so craves, he gives up in despair, wastes away – or drowns, depending on which version one is reading. Perhaps the feminists are correct in supposing that he would never get back to the idealised womb. But he can't leave the pool since he is not getting the necessary confirmation which will release him.

In emotional and motivational terms the Narcissus myth has generated ideas that have fascinated philosophers, psychologists, sociologists, feminists, artists and poets, who have used its theme like clay that can be shaped into any number of pots, figurines and abstract forms according to the whim of the ceramicist.

Emphasis shifts: one hundred years after Ovid, Pausanias pours cold water on the idea that anyone could have been so silly as to fail to recognise themselves and fall in love with their own reflection – what Narcissus must have seen was the reflection of his twin sister who had drowned in the mirror pool. Poor Echo gets airbrushed out of the story, which is a pity because in spite of her speech defect she is the only one who offers Narcissus the chance of a genuine relationship, her unconditional love. For it is only in relationship that the endless quest for confirmation comes to rest, the boundaries dissolve as we become 'part of', taking root in and growing through each other. Our inner self resonates in shared Being.

The Narcissus story is easy to misread as Narcissus looking 'at' himself (in admiration) rather than 'for' his lost self. Confusion arises from the two different interpretations of self; that of superficial appearance and inner quality, to the extent that nowadays it is easy to allow endless 'selfies' to fast track us into what is aptly described as the 'quagmire of narcissism'[121].

The story twists and turns but what it does show is that we can reach out a very long distance in the search for confirmation of our identity. Leaping centuries, the Surrealists seized on the metamorphic implications of the Narcissus myth, crystallised in a spectacular self portrait by Salvador Dali, with a narcissus flower impaled on each of the spurs of his handlebar moustache. He paints a powerful picture of the drowning hand of Narcissus grasping a cracked egg from which a flowering Narcissus bulb emerges. Hoping that Freud would endorse his view of transformation of unconscious activity, Dali took this with him when he went to see Freud in London. The visit was not a success. 'In what I alleged to have rung the death-knoll of surrealist art, Freud disappointed him, telling Dali that while he acknowledges the power of the painting, in classical art he looks for operations of the unconscious – but that in a surrealism, he sees only those of the conscious[122].

---

121 Pullman L (2017) 'I'm in a Hot New Social Network; Its Real Life.' *Sunday Times.* **30 August.**

122 Lomas D (2011) *'Narcissus Reflected: The myth of Narcissus in Surrealist and Contemporary Art'.* Published by Fruitmarket Gallery Edinburgh

Chapter 15: A gradient of consciousness?

Graziano suggests that our awareness of our self is an illusion played by the brain, which puts together sensations felt by the body, building mind-maps to construct itself an internal self-model, 'which keeps track of whatever is being controlled, allows for predictions and planning – and then looks at it'[123]?

Linnaeus decided that insects have no brains. Leaping a few generations, Graziano says that even if they do, the insect brain is too small for a sense of self: invertebrates lack the wherewithal to do much more than simply react to sensations[124].

In licensing myself to borrow from insects only remotely connected with scarabs, I am trying to unravel a contradiction, in that, even if insects do have very small brains, at least some of them appear to have the potential to evolve sophisticated behaviour, more than might be anticipated if they were simply reacting without thought. Take the Marshmallow test, a psychological investigative tool that measures the development of self-control in children. Each child is offered one marshmallow but told they can have two if they wait for a quarter of an hour.

Left alone to ponder the alternatives, the question is will she, presuming she likes marshmallows, opt for 'the bird in hand that is worth two in the bush' and grab the treat, or wait out temptation, delaying gratification in favour of the bigger prize. (I have always thought that the flaw in this experiment is the nature of the incentive, which needs to be rather more inviting than a bland pink or white puffball of marshmallow; chocolate perhaps?)

According to Mischel[125], fMRI scans suggest that yielding to immediate temptation relates to activity in the more primitive limbic system but the ability to exercise self-control and hang on for the big prize involves the frontal cortex. Which is interesting, because an investigation into self-control in black ants (which lack a large frontal brain), shows these invertebrates have evolved similar self-control[126]. That is, having learned from another ant of a large reward further away from the nest, they will walk twice as far – and expend twice as much energy – for a big dollop of sugar instead of stopping off to snack at the smaller pile close to the nest. (The insects are thought to exchange this information through behaviour called trophallaxis, which looks like kissing but is a form of social vomiting[127]).

123 Graziano M (2016)'Consciousness: The Mind Messing With the Mind' *The Atlantic*. **7 April.**

124 Graziano M (2016) 'A New Theory Explains how Consciousness Evolved' *The Atlantic*. **6 June.**

125 Mischel W (2015) 'The Marshmallow Test: Mastering Self-Control'

126 Moody O (2017) How ants have learned to pay the waiting game. *The Times*. **11 October.**

127 Wendt S and Czaczkes T, Individual ant workers show self-control. Royal Society Biology Letters 11 October 2017.DOI: 10.1098/rsbl.2017.0450

Insects perform surprisingly well in constructing mental maps of their surroundings and even, in the case of bees, to transmit them to other bees through their dance at the mouth of the hive. Desert ants building nests from leaves can find their way walking backwards, with an occasional glance backwards to check up on direction.

Feinberg continues, the only thing that really matters is whether the insect can form mental images. He describes an experiment in which bees learn to identify and memorise one of a number of gate patterns which lead to a concealed target pattern, beyond which is food. 'They had put the gate pattern image into memory and then related it to the correct target pattern.' They had formed a visual image, implying sensory consciousness, at least in bees[128].

As well as Feinberg's first level of consciousness it is becoming clear that some insects (possibly including the scarab family) also experience a second level of consciousness: a kind of half-way house between exteroceptive perception (interpreting what is going on outside impinges on them) and the ability to feel emotions. Messages may refer both to the inner body and external environment. They may be experienced as local mental images and also as inner visceral and affective states.

Anatomically, while they may have small brains, insects are in possession of the necessary bits of the three-part midbrain necessary for subjective experience which enables them, when in motion, to form a nerve map of their state in space:

'a basic awareness of the world without further reflection on that awareness. This is considered the most basic form of consciousness. Tellingly, this capacity is supported by the integrated midbrain and basal ganglia structures, which are among the oldest and most highly conserved brain systems in vertebrates. A reasonable inference is that the capacity for subjective experience is both widespread and evolutionarily old within the vertebrate lineage. We argue that the insect brain supports functions analogous to those of the vertebrate midbrain and hence that insects may also have a capacity for subjective experience.'[129]

And they score surprisingly high up the scale in other requirements, performing a wide range of behaviours, showing behavioural flexibility and the ability to learn. But from the point of view of the evolution of self-awareness, are they conscious of what they sense? Does the maybug really know what she is doing or is she simply 'following her nose', carrying on regardless in response to external stimuli and the internal stimuli that are the consequences of these (fear, for example) but not being able to reflect on these experiences.

We are on the borders of self-awareness. Smell is critical. When the maybug grubs sniff out food underground and when, as adults, they pick up chemicals from damaged leaves and head towards them in search of a mate who may be munching them, are they responding in the same way as a plant growing towards the light? As far as we know no conscious decisions have been taken. Or have they? Does the maybug feel, 'Ah yum-yum', when it moves towards the

---

128 ibid.

129 Klein C & Barron AB. (2016). Insects have the capacity for subjective experience. *Animal sentience* **1**(9) 1-19.

smell of damaged oak leaves but not when it smells macerated potato? Does this begin to border on a choice to move (involving the expenditure of energy), or not, or is it simply a response to evolutionary imperative, in the sense that one option is more life supporting than another.

Again, Maybugs approaches obstacles like a tank; she crashes into them (as far as windows and people are concerned) and if this does not remove the hazard, she goes round its edge until she finds a way through and then continues on the same course. All of which suggest that once she has set her sat-nav according to her needs she is reluctant to deviate. But this lack of flexibility is combined in her first cousin the scarab with a certain amount of cunning when the male attempts to steal another scarab's bigger better dung ball.

It is difficult to conceive that Scarab A, intent on rustling a larger dung ball from Scarab B who is struggling to overcome an obstacle, waits for a opportunity to carry out his attack without having some sort of mental image of his intention, or at least positive valence of the 'this is good for me' variety. To us, the whole operation seems to imply the capacity for planning and deceit. But it is easy to slip into projecting our human feelings into the insect, creating a false 'I' to whom we can relate.

Scarabs who do successfully make off with better dung balls are more likely to perpetuate their genes. And if my doomed Maybugs does have feelings in the sense of emotions, are they anything more than some elaborately programmed instinct which will take her to the garden on the other side of the lane where there may be food and shelter?

Essentially, what do maybugs and their cousins 'feel' when they react to threat – do they know fear – and from a first person perspective, feel an 'I' which reflects on being afraid[130]?

What is clear is that the maybug is in no sense a drone, an automaton in action only at the behest of a living other, or a pre-programmed robot. She has life, a 'being aliveness' that we share. And while, since her flight paths are circumscribed by biological imperative and manipulated by circumstances, she cannot just drop everything and take off on holiday, she is not radio controlled by another living creature for their own purposes. She can make choices, although she operates within the limitations of her biological niche. And in what sense is the scarab conscious of the readings it takes from the constellations during its orientation dance, presumably committing them to some sort of recorded flight plan, since she can resume the same trajectory after negotiating an obstacle?

Do the mushroom bodies account for the more sophisticated layers of apparently conscious behaviour in insects? Taking insects overall, recent investigations into the neuroanatomy of mutant flies which lack mushroom bodies, confirms that they are key players in learning and in the formation and storage of memories. In cockroaches, lesions in the mushroom bodies

130 Klein C & Barron A (April 19th 2016) 'Insects can teach us about the origins of consciousness' http://phys.org/news/2016-04-insects-consciousness.html (accessed April 2019)

impair their ability to find a hidden target[131]. And if we take the scarab on the slippery slope of the sand dune, after fruitless efforts he learns that he cannot reach his goal and gives up trying in favour of a new behaviour (fly off and find a better venue).

So if we humans rule out reflex actions that happen without our taking conscious decisions, are we any further on in understanding what we mean when we talk about consciousness, self-awareness and awareness of the state of being?

Now that, using scanners, we can watch what is happening in the brain while we are thinking about, for example, a visual experience, we are beginning to be able to relate sensory intake to neuronal activity. We can see where the action is in the primary visual cortex. People who have severed their spinal cord, or even damaged the small and most ancient part of our brain (the cerebellum), report little change in their ability to experience subjective sensations[132]. Koch says that in order for us to be conscious of our intake, rather than neurons which simply pass messages from one nerve to the next as in the cerebellum, we need the complicated neuronal networks that involve feedback loops and are found in the deeply folded (and more recent) outer surface of the brain in the cerebral cortex.

Can I make a conscious choice? Contrary to what I have believed to be the case, most of my decisions are dictated by unconscious promptings. While these are not the same as involuntary reactions (which do not involve the brain), and while I feel myself to be consciously making a choice, in reality they are the outcome of unconscious arbitration between different directives in my brain.

Using TMS (Transcranial Magnetic Stimulation) to send an electrical stimulus across a specific area of the brain, Professor Pascual-Leone asked a subject to look at a computer screen. When the light was red, they had to make up their mind as to which hand they would lift up – a simple choice – but not to act on it. When the light was yellow, a burst of TMS was sent through the brain. When the light turned green, they had to move the hand they had chosen. Professor Pascual-Leone showed that, by using TMS, it was possible to get the subject to change their mind while still being absolutely convinced that they had made a conscious choice. In reality, the TMS was triggering the change of mind. Questionnaires made it clear that the subject remained convinced that they had made a free-will choice. Although this is in an early stage of research, the implication may be that unconscious intention precedes conscious action; consequently, although my brain is larger than hers and contains many, many more unconscious circuits to argue the outcome, my so-called free will choices may not be totally unlike those made by Maybugs.

Interpretations of experiments such as these are being argued hotly but what does emerge is that the on/off switch for consciousness is likely to have evolved in response to evolutionary requirements wherever they appear, rather than a smooth gradient.

Maybugs has brought me this far; an interesting companion, she has fed

---

131 Davis LR Kyung-An Han Neuroanatomy: Mushrooming Mushroom Bodies. *Science Direct* **6** (2) pp146-148

132 Koch C 'What is Consciousness?' Scientific American.com. June 2018

me with ideas and led me into territories that I should not have explored on my own. While I am deeply indebted to her, somewhere along the gradient of consciousness we are going to have to part company, at least for the time being, since I need to press on to the top of the ridge and see what's on the other side.

Chapter 16: Self awareness

Feinberg's third level of consciousness is a step up – where we don't just feel emotions but reflect on them so that they contribute to our awareness of our self. We are self-aware. To do this we are going to need a wrap round, cerebral cortex to enable us to reflect on our experiences.

An abstract print by the artist Jane Bluiell called 'Compartments' hangs on my wall. Soft gold and blue, it has the embroidered quality of an antique tapestry. Its subject is the alternative versions of our selves we present to different people. On the left, what appears to be a semi-permeable membrane separates a number of spheres in a vague undermind from the outside world. One or two have managed to escape to the right. Underlying our personal friendships there is an urgent search for confirmation. So the face with which we engage one person can present differently to another. If we are honest with ourselves, however unconsciously, most of us try to match ourselves to our friends by putting forward that aspect of our selves which we think they may find attractive. In this sense we are chameleons, adopting the colour of our immediate surroundings.

This is surreal territory, where one finds oneself conscious of self on the one hand, but also having to reflect that this self is built on sand, having no basis in whatever it is we call real. With the possible exception of 'The Hunting of the Snark', default is set to void. Lewis Carroll's poem is a surreal account of a motley crew of men (no women) who, led by the Bellman whose navigational skills left much to be desired, set out across a blank map to find the Snark, an animal that turns out to be a dangerous Boojum (who would softly and silently disappear the hunter). Kelly interprets the poem as 'Carroll's comic rendition of his fears of disorder and chaos, with the comedy serving as a psychological defence against the devastating idea of personal annihilation'. It does not seem to stretch the imagination too far to suggest that the Bellman's assorted companions represent aspects of the poet's personality; the bold and the timid, the skilful and the ham-fisted, the autocrat, the pet, the dreamer and the absent minded to the point of dementia.

Humorous defence against existential darkness or search for self: perhaps they are the same thing? We are all part of a lucky dip. And I am acquainted with the idea of an elusive self as a Snark, who turns out to be a Boojum and is able to dematerialise at the drop of a hat: sounds familiar.

Time to heave my non-existence out of this philosophical cul-de-sac, and start to enjoy the on-loan (if bogus), material manifestation that is me thinking about myself – and you thinking about yourself.

Firstly, I want to set aside self-consciousness, which is easily confused with self-awareness – but self-consciousness implies that we are thinking about ourselves in relation to what others think about us (usually comparing ourselves unfavourably).

Separated from the outside world only by a thin layer of skin, our cranium is the nearest we humans get to an exoskeleton, the rampart that protects everything that is meaningful to us. We take it for granted to the extent that it is almost shocking to listen to Thomas Bewick, the famous nineteenth century wood engraver, describing sitting by the opened grave of his father holding his skull in his hands. He moulds his father's temples, meditates as his fingers retracing its bumps and hollows with affection. (As a small boy, one can imagine him riding on his shoulders, holding tight to his head, feeling the shape of his bones.) Far from being macabre, his sadness is embodied in acceptance and love. His emotions are physically part of his identity. Although he is reflecting on them, they are part of who he is[133].

So, setting aside the science, given that I am not only conscious but am speculating about how a stimulus feels, how do I get from consciousness and self-awareness to a sense of 'myself as I', this is me, this is my flavour? After all, you and I may see the same thing but extrapolate a totally different affective experience, depending on what we associate with it. Different from our awareness of our sensory needs or even of reflection on our affective states, my self awareness is the dynamic statement of my existence, rather than the agent of responsiveness. We attend to ourselves. And the Romanian poet Paul Celan says, 'Attentiveness is the natural prayer of the soul'[134]. Aware even as we are afraid to look, we guard 'I' closely from ourselves. This is the I that both speaks and is uttered.

How can I bear to look at the sky and admit that what I see goes on forever, when it is more comfortable to imagine it as the upturned lid of a soup tureen? It is easier to come to terms with an image than with an abstraction. I need something concrete to hold on to. Under these circumstances, the question of whether or not my personal identity is an illusion becomes irrelevant, since it at least it provides me with a façade of stability, something to hang on to.

Most of us humans associate having a feeling of ourselves with knowing our flavour, quiddity, who we are and what this means in terms of being able to reflect on it and possessing the ability to respond. This is not achieved without struggle, since the pathway to having a sense of self is booby-trapped with our capacity to project feelings we don't fancy and introject those that rightly belong elsewhere. Once we have rejected our negative feelings we do not have to take responsibility for them, or the consequences of our failure to own these. On the other hand adopting attitudes that we would like to be ours can mask who we really are, not only from others but also from ourselves. However there are times when the mask acts as a mould so that behaving 'as if' becomes habitual. Most hazardous of all is psychological inertia, drifting through a second-hand world.

Early memories of self-awareness, the feeling of being me, relate to physical sensations: the stiff hairiness of my father's Harris tweed jacket smells oily

133 Bewick T. Encyclopedia of the Romantic Era 1760-1850 Vol.1 & 2. Ed, Christopher John Murray p.87

134 Kafka and the Golem - Translating Paul Celan. *Prooftexts* **6** (2) pp172-183.

and tickles my nose as he piggybacks me up the field. And on all fours, the rough grain of granite garden steps is even now printed in my knees' memory as I hoisted them over the lip, stood up and tottered along the top of a wall. A new perspective opened up to a distant pond, and I am looking over the cloche hat of my accompanying Nanny, pushing an empty pram. I can hear her voice now, 'come down Miss Phoebe-Ann at once'. In spite of being informed that this recollection has a 40% chance of being false (since the developing brain lacks capacity for such early memory), or at most an assemblage of fragmentary experiences, this one can be dated, since the glasshouse in the background was later pulled down. These are simple sensory recollections of a world outside – but this thing I call 'I' is an affective participant. The I that know now is a component part of them.

Perception of a defined self as such comes via my sister, who caught me looking at myself in a long mirror (aged three) admiring my dress and saying, 'I think I should like a pink one, with blue buttons and yellow bows'. I cannot defend my emerging aesthetic sense.

Me as an abstract concept came with Billie Holliday and the song, 'Me, Myself and I'. By 1940, the time I arrived at school, the title had morphed, so we sang 'My, My, Myself and I'. 'My' is clearly the odd word out, a transition between the essence of me-ness and those things which I consider to be extensions of 'me', my pen, my house, my car, even as I drove past it this morning, my Ash tree, on the left hand side of the A65 into which I crashed a year ago. Starting with my corporeal outline, my shape is intact, I can run my hands over it and recognise its features. But since I am not wearing a suit of armour, my 'My' is continuant, reaching out from my flesh to invest in my personal space, the add-on within which I feel safe – and which can feel invaded if you enter without invitation. And my particular personal space is cluttered with possessions: this is an area in which I have an interest.

But it's not just my personal possessions: I am equally defensive of my 'is he one of us' psychological landscape as I am of the physical limits of my body. You there outside me have a problem here, in that my personal sensitivities are not always well demarcated, so it's easy for you to trample on inner motivations that have somehow leaked into personal space.

In a large hall I am trying to give a small group of students conscious awareness of what this intangible extension of self feels like. I push the six chairs together in a huddle in the middle so they are touching. The first thing the students do is move the chairs apart. When I ask them why, they look embarrassed. They do not like to say they feel uncomfortable sitting so close to their neighbours, to admit to the feeling of invasion. (There is always an exception, in this case a group of four, happily cemented together in an island in the middle. When I comment, they laugh and say, 'Oh, we like cozying up to each other'. They have an unusual sense of themselves as a collective).

Beyond this, I can send feelers to tap the boundaries of perception, to my environment, even my planet, but cannot go on wandering space forever without dilution. It is partly a question of how many numbers I can assemble in my mind's eye before the brain gives up, ten, a hundred, a thousand, by clumping thousands together, possibly even a million – but coming to billions I have to use the symbol, 'n' to rein in the number of noughts and make them manageable.

Raising my eyes to beyond, there is infinity, a relaxed figure of eight, lying on one side and taking its ease. Looping the loop gently, endless in all directions, Bertrand Russell describes the lemniscate as 'immeasurably subtle and profound'[135]. Here my personal quest for boundary and confirmation comes to a full stop; there really is nowhere else to go.

Sadly, mathematicians are busy disrupting this oceanic nirvana, suggesting there is more than one infinity, dependent on whether they are pursuing a countable or an uncountable pathway to its power[136]. The image of a quiescent lemniscate is hotting up: wriggling like a Mobius strip, it twists and turns in an attempt to iron out its kink.

The world is changing. Back here from the stars, 'Me and My', are quivering in a flow of self-confirming ego-centricity, feeding ourselves on a diet of Facebook and Amazon algorhythms, catering to our insatiable need for confirmation. We no longer have to reach outside ourselves for validation since iPads and smart phones provide us with pseudo-exoskeletons, in the sense that we do not have to reach out for confirmation.

But as we endlessly search social media for a mirage audience (that divorces us from the 'Who' that we are), our psychological confirmation of self and our very sense of existence trails behind. 'We keep swiping and swiping because we are never satisfied'[137] (we are not contained in ourselves but must seek external confirmation). For all our cyber-cruising, what we set up is the empty promise of a disembodied mirror, an illusion that may tell us our server is at work but does not add to our physical sense of self. Delivered by drone, we find what we are looking for and it turns out to be sterile, lacking empathy. Narcissus comes to a solitary end.

The whole world is mine: except it isn't. On the contrary, it belongs to all of us equally, so, like Maybugs, we are in competition for limited resources. Ditch the iPhone in order to survive, I am going to have to relate to the world outside myself, indeed my psychological survival is dependent on my capacity to empathise.

135 Wikipedia https://en.wikipedia.org/wiki/infinity#CITEREFRussell1996_[1903]
136 Whipple T (2017) The Riddle of Infinity. *The Times* **15 September**
137 Sullivan A (2016) Switch Off. *Sunday Times* **27 November**

Chapter 17: The search for real

(Note to Maybugs: Look, I know I am keeping you waiting but I promise it will not be that long. I will take you to the Death Café and we will collect some oak leaves on the way, as I suspect you will prefer them to butter-cream buns. Meanwhile give me a wave with one of your blade-banner flanges, just so I know you are still around.)

At the risk of repetition, because this is so crucial to the argument, we literally learn about our physical selves through contact with others. When I see you, I not only pick up information about how you are feeling, but a second message to my brain tells me my eyes are in working order (or not). When you speak to me, I not only hear what you say, but my brain gets the message that my ears are in working order – and so on for all the senses. It is through my contacts with you that I learn about my physical self. I am embodied through relationship. And it is not only my physical self that is apparent, I learn from your reactions about my emotional responses, reflected in your facial and body language.

So why bother with introspection, since the path to finding one's own flavour (to be able to read one's own identity tag) is hard work? It is relatively easy to cruise along, especially in these days of instant entertainment, judging one's worth by how many 'likes' one can acquire, without looking inwards. Why bother to search for who I am, when my smartphone, together with Twitter and Facebook and all the other paraphernalia of the internet are functionally in hand: instant confirmation and panaceas to aloneness? What are the dangers of psychological inertia?

To assess the affect of compulsive interaction with interactive modern technology, the sociologist Sherry Turkle interviewed hundreds of people of all ages. She reminds us of how easy it is to lose our capacity for solitude and self-discovery, together with first-hand relationships. We start to treat people as objects[138]. She goes on to say, 'the current position seems to be that if there is a robot that can fool me into thinking that it understands me, I'm good to have it as a companion'. In an interview, she takes this further: 'to where documenting becomes the reason for living – the pursuit becomes the purpose'. As a contemporary reinterpretation of Descartes, she proposes:

'I document, therefore I am'[139].

Or I can have a robot to comfort me. But robo-confirmation is counterfeit and the robot is a program, delivering second-hand empathy. Are we this easily

---

138 Sherry Turkle, interviewed by Mark Fischetti in *Scientific American Special Edition* Autumn 2016

139 Fischetti M. Interview with Sherry Turkle, 'How selfie culture is changing our lives'. *Scientific American.*

fooled? To know one's self is to be open to all of oneself, to acknowledge one's weaknesses and feel comfortable with one's strengths: above all, to know one's own flavour. It's like living in colour rather than in black and white, reading an Ordinance Survey map rather than being directed by Sat-Nav.

So how do we traverse the gulf from consciousness to a feeling of who we are, the me that is not just my superficial appearance as a clothes-horse for celebrity fashion, but rather the psychological shape of the person I-self that is doing the feeling, my inscape looking out. Self-awareness requires solitude and needs to be embodied. Not all of us are as good at this as we might like to think.

And in a world that is increasingly lived online, the odds of finding ourselves and experiencing internalisation and self discovery are increasingly stacked against us. If we are not satisfied with our image we can build ourselves an avatar, which will compensate for our deficiencies. We can physically feel through our avatar.

It is so easy to become alienated from reality by the lure of artificial technology. Since one of the themes of this book is mortality, take the example of grief:

'Build your own agent' is an app that will allow us to 'talk to the dead', feeding the dead person's text messages into a Google programme to create personalised chat bots – computer programs designed to simulate conversation between the departed and their mourners[140]. Its creator, Eugenia Kuyda, rationalises, 'it's not about pretending someone is alive, it's about accepting it and thinking and talking about it and not staying in denial'. (What are friends and neighbours for?) Eugenia continues, 'young people do not have a way to deal with death any more – you go to the funeral and then go back to work and get on with it.' (She is mistaken, this is not just a problem for the young, for those left behind death has always been about putting your head down and getting on with grief.)

The entrepreneur spots a gap in the market. 'Everyone dies, lots of grief. How about we go into personalised comfort?' Really? Listen.

'Experts predict that companies could soon offer to create bereavement chat bots for customers amid growing interest in how technology can be used to help people deal with death'[141].

And Paul Armstrong of Here/Forth, a technology advisory company, says, 'This sort of technology is likely to become commercialised … there's a lot of activity in the digital death market already – for example, websites that lets you send video messages after you die'[142].

Real life is harsh but I want to be who I am. It is the only defence I have in an indifferent environment. Finding my essential is a journey of self-examination without judgement, stripping off projections and letting go of introjections; acknowledging that which belongs and relinquishing what I have borrowed. In order to do this I have to learn to look at my emotions

140 Mark Bridge 'Good Grief: Keep talking to friends beyond the Grave' *The Times* **11 October**

141 ibid.

142 See Here Forth Technology: http://www.hereforth.com (accessed April 2019)

and feelings full on, following the pain, seeking its roots. If I am able to bring this to consciousness, the affective onslaught is blunted – although still present, it no longer dictates my behaviour. My quiddity emerges; I no longer ask, 'who am I?', but know myself as 'I am'. Self. Even if I am an artifact, I am the realest thing I've got.

So perhaps it is just me, but the idea, and even more so the marketing of bereavement bots is a step not just too far, but right over the edge of the precipice, not just of taste but of psychological damage.

The reason for my vigorous distaste is that we learn and grow through the process of grieving. Yes it hurts but it also changes us. To deliberately engage with an artificial construct is to build on a false premise and place an obstacle in the way of internalisation. The more ingenious our self-deception the further we separate ourselves from everything that is authentic, or what we think of as authentic.

Even so, perhaps we should ask ourselves what is the difference between self-confirmation – as practiced when, for example, we pat our hair to reassure ourselves (or if we are autistic, use a repetitive behaviour to tell ourselves who we are) – and the wishful thinking of the memorial bot, even when used with the best intentions? This is not quite so simple to answer as one might imagine.

If one responds to the sounds of a non-verbal child with autism, using the language that has meaning for them, they will often interact, while a recording of their sounds played back may initially arouse their interest, but this usually flags as they realise they are not being answered in a relevant manner. To be effective and affective, a response must offer contingency. But given sufficient text messages fed into the Google programme, this appears to be a technical possibility, although we are warned that the virtual agent needs to sound conversational to be convincing. What is missing is the agency and spontaneity of the absent person on which to build new constructs, rather than just fill in the missing bricks. What is on offer is psychological Polyfilla, potentially damaging to the process of embracing grief and coming to terms with the death of a person one loves, allowing them to be gone and our wound to heal.

The journey to knowing one's self is more than just egoistical self-absorption, we cannot know other people in all their fascinating diversity if we are projecting our feelings on to them. All we are doing is creating a mirror for ourselves: a falsie in which we see what we want to see, what we can bear, in our own reflection. To live without knowing who we are, is to exist like a Water-Boatman, skittering across the meniscus of empathy.

To revert to the first person, when I have learned to live with myself as I am, there is no longer any need to distort my perception of you with projections on you of the bits of me I cannot carry – nor to warp myself by taking on board and feeling parts of you as myself. Beyond what I know of myself as I, there is you, you unadulterated by my needs and desires; a new landscape waiting to be explored.

So how do we go about it?

Communication is not just about swapping words, it's about engaging with feelings. I want to talk to you because I need to be able to swap information, but just as importantly I need confirmation of my existence. When I interact with you, will you treat me as subject rather than object and will you show me what I am doing? 'I' wants to be 'we,' because we is potentially a stronger unit than I on its own. In particular, I needs to know if it trusts you, and if you will promote its existence. Is I safe with you?

I am in a primary school in North London. The catchment area is ethnically diverse. The immediate setting is appallingly noisy; next door to a building site with diggers and earth-movers excavating several basements down at full throttle. In the foyer I am welcomed with the information that there are 19 languages in the school – pause for effect – and this is only in the staff room. In the school, there are around 90 plus, that is if you count the different dialects. Clearly, there is an in-house communication problem.

Fortunately, since I was not even able to master French at school, I am here to work using body language with children who have no speech. Autistic and confused, they are drifting around banging plastic bottles, playing with shadows, crying in the corner, sitting by the door trying to escape. With the best will in the world, the staff are unable to make contact with them. In effect, the curriculum does not offer them the tools to engage their attention.

There are two ways in which you and I can communicate with each other. The first is Functional Communication, the exchange of information through speech, although the boundaries of speech are becoming blurred with the increasing availability of information online. Why bother to go and see someone when you can text them? The alternative is Emotional Engagement through observation of body language. We watch each other all the time.

There are many books about the use of body language (mainly to control your partner), which itemise positions – if you have your arms folded across your chest you are being defensive and so on. What I am talking about is more than this: intimate attention to your quiddity using all my senses. This is an engagement which involves empathy, rather than postural observation. I have to empty myself and be there for you.

And in order for us to interact, we have to use signals that have meaning for each other. Even if I could resurrect Maybugs, it would be useless to speak to her, since her capacity to hear is questionable and her vision probably too pixillated to have detailed understanding. And it would be difficult to use body language with a creature in armor. What I should have to offer her is the delicious smell of crushed oak roots or leaves. It is difficult to see how these diffuse experiences could be anything more than a lure, even if it draws her towards a food source, or possibly towards a potential mate who was crushing oak leaves as she munched.

As well as offering signals that have meaning, our initiatives and responses have to be presented in such a way as that they are accessible to the recipient. Meet Lenny, who has an intellectual disability. I am told he is difficult: sometimes he responds to sign language and at other times he ignores it. I watch him carefully. It becomes obvious that he does respond to signs when the sender is standing in front of him, but not if they are standing at one side or the other. Lenny has tunnel vision: his visual field is restricted and what he can see is limited to an area you or I would see if we looked down the tube of a toilet roll. Because his staff have complete visual fields, they are interpreting his negative responses according to their own sensory perception, projecting their sensory experience onto him and blaming him for laziness.

In emptying of ourselves of our own agenda and entering the world of our conversation partner we learn what is important for them and this begins to take on deeper meaning for us. A bead is no longer just a bead: it has colour and density, it bounces – and reflects light in a particular way. In some ways this is trivial but in others it opens up our senses to qualia (the intense essence of a quality) in a deeper way. We realise what we are missing: it is like moving from black and white to colour vision. What is at first simple exchange, becomes engagement and flow. Both parties are participant.

My eyes are opened to this form of engagement (now known as Intensive Interaction[143]), when I am sacked from a hospital that has decided to focus on Age Appropriateness and Normalization, irrespective of what meets the needs of and has meaning for the people to whom it is applied. In a hospital for people with 'Mental Handicap', as it was then called, the staff decided to cheer up the ward with ornaments on the mantelpiece, which were promptly destroyed by the autistic residents. Determined to fulfill the criteria of a 'normal' environment, and irrespective of the clearly expressed wishes of those who had to live with what for them were perceived as threatening distractions, the staff bought a second batch and stuck them down with superglue. Gail Gillingham offers a greater understanding of the Autistic condition – 'People with autism need visual and auditory tranquility'[144].

Garry Ephraim was my supervisor for four years when I held a Joseph Rowntree Fellowship. He changed my life as I learned to use body language, non-verbal sounds and mime to tune into the emotional world of people with whom we struggle to communicate. I say 'we' because it is as difficult for us to talk to them as it is for them to talk to us. I learned to focus on the inner world of those whose disablement bars them from telling us what they want, and more importantly, how they feel.

This is a new way of perceiving the world, not just through intellect but learning to value what 'me' and 'not me' feel together, what we spark off in each other; a way of interaction I had somehow overlooked. Perhaps it is because adults instinctively associate this intuitive communication with mother and baby interactions and are afraid of being thought to be childish. But in rejecting this gift of understanding, we also set aside profound insight into the worlds of those we meet: in doing so we impoverish ourselves.

143 As a way of engaging attention, Intensive Interaction (as it is now known) was introduced as a method by the Clinical Psychologist Geraint Ephraim in the 1980s. Originally called Augmented Mothering, it was rejected by the then current favorite approach of Normalisation and Age Appropriateness. Renamed by Nind and Hewett, Intensive Interaction is now used round the world and is a successful way of engaging attention with non-verbal adults and children.

144 Gail Gillingham (2001) *Autism – Handle with Care*. Tacit Press

In practice it is not just about following what other people are doing but about a reciprocal conversation without words; a way in to sharing our worlds and a direct link to emotional warmth. Once we put aside our own agendas, it is easy, natural, and happens in commonplace ways. A reciprocal warmth is implanted in us and we become part of each other's experience.

Unsurprisingly, we have inherited these communicative skills from the animal kingdom. If we learn their language we can talk to them. Birds communicate through their calls and we do not have to be St Frances to join in, even on Skype. Two beautiful scarlet and green king parrots are chirruping as they gobble seed on the balcony table of a friend in Australia, so I respond. Immediately the female's head comes up as she fixes me with her round eye, with total attention. Chirruping in turns, we continue to talk to each other across oceans and continents.

It is not just sound. If geese are alarmed, they will charge with extended necks and puffed up wing feathers, making themselves look bigger and more intimidating. They back off quickly when I adopt a similar profile, head low and forward, with my arms aligned down my side and rattling away from my body so as to enlarge my silhouette. Now I am a bigger goose and they turn tail and run, squawking indignantly. Even a starling responds when I walk beneath a telegraph wire and answer her calls. Her head follows me round, to the extent she loses her balance and falls off the wire.

Body language conversations are effective with horses, dogs, cats and cows, although heavy breathing interactions with cattle are more difficult now that farmers remove calves from their mother's at birth. Perhaps they never really get a chance to learn their mother tongue. Sheep are not very responsive unless they are hungry – it is sometimes possible to engage with their lambs, that is until the ewe intervenes: she guards her offspring diligently, recalling them with a swift bleat if she considers they are becoming too intimate with a stranger.

Finally, there is a delicious nose-to-nose conversation between David Attenborough and a half-blind baby rhinoceros calling to each other on YouTube, guaranteed to extract a maternal, 'Aaahhh': extraordinary how widely spread the maternal instinct is.

To summarise: self to self, body language opens the door to understanding the emotions of each other, to empathising with how each other feels. We reveal our inner attitudes and vulnerabilities in reciprocal interactions, even if even are not consciously aware of it. How we get on with each other depends on how good we are at reading each other's body language. We are looking at how people are expressing their initiatives, rather than copying exactly what they are doing, using gestures and sounds and rhythms that their brain understands immediately without elaborate processing. Given the difficulties that some autistic people have with visual processing this means they are surprisingly good at picking up on our responses. We know if each other's responses are welcoming or hostile, since it is through our posture, stance, facial language and prosody that we learn about each other's affective state and intentions.

At this point I am cross-examined by a friend – how does this relate to the different aspects of our personality emerging in the tapestry picture? How do we know if we are meeting with an essential person or distortions, however unintentional? How do we identify the spurious from the real? I walk back into the sitting room, plant myself on the sofa, put my feet up and soak myself in the intention of the artist. What is she trying to say?

I am looking for quiddity, the real thing – all the others are a cover up, attempts to present myself in the best light, displacements that adopt the language of and model their attitudes on those of the other person. This is not so much deliberate deception as an attempt to attract favorable attention, for whatever reason. Of course it can be negative, defensive – or you or I could be on a power trip, deliberately seeking to manipulate the other. But perhaps it is not so much a different persona that is being offered, as that as we emerge we defend our weaknesses, skillfully manipulating our surroundings so that we appear in the most favorable light. This is a basic biological behavior; we need allies in order to survive.

So how can we differentiate between the authentic voice and an adopted self, both in our relationship to others and, as importantly, in ourselves? Perhaps the search for authenticity is a will-o-the-wisp, forever chasing the unattainable. Maybe, maybe not. But the more we are able to strip ourselves of our acquired psychological baggage, the closer we get the core; even if we do not find it, we know it is there. We are warmed by it, to the point where we find ourselves, however vulnerable, acting from it, rather than trying to disguise our true selves. This is where our flavor is spoken as much as speaks: poets call it finding the Voice.

Both in finding ourselves and when we are reading the body language of others, we have to abandon analysis in favor of insight, since the only way we can tell the difference is by focusing on the niggling feeling that there is a misfit. It is as though the other person is wearing the wrong dress, perhaps one that will attract attention but does not look right on them. We have to let the discomfort in this intuitive inkling be our guide. And it seems likely that the more we allow our true voice to speak, the less we have to search for external confirmation. It is not that, like Maybugs, we have acquired an external skeleton off which to bounce our needs, but rather that we now have an inner source of knowing our being.

All of which is apparent when we pay intimate attention to body language and come close to each other. Now I know what you are feeling and you know what I am feeling. Empathy becomes 'as one' with you.

I was talking to a training group about this extraordinary bonding that can develop between two people engaged in a body language conversation, when a young man who I thought had been asleep spoke up from the back row. 'I know what you're on about, you're talking about flow.'

Flamenco dancers have a special word to describe the flow between them, 'duende'. Duende is a quality, the resonance that makes a performance unforgettable. It occurs when a partner is inhabited, possessed by a force or set of compulsions coming from outside her or his own self. 'Duende…

is unforgettable because it visits the present in order to address the future[145].' We confirm our embodied self in other than ourselves: each dancer is simultaneously aware of themselves and the other, of holding and being held, not necessarily physically. This is flow: one could not insert a piece of psychological tissue paper between the two.

Confirmation is critical for self-perception, for knowing what we are seeing and hearing and feeling. We need to know what and who we are, so we are constantly seeking to confirm this self-image throughout our lives and looking to top up this sensory reaffirmation, either by self-stimulus or reaching out for more. Repeated confirmation using one sense to check up on another reinforces neural pathways and our general picture we have of ourselves. Importantly, our soft human boundaries may mean we have to go a long way out of our fleshly limits to find the validation we need to prop up our sense of self.

Inside her cuirass, Maybugs may have less need to reach out for proprioceptive confirmation than those of us with soft edges – she has it on tap. Sadly, and in spite of filling my mind with ideas, it is at least in part her rigidity that makes it impossible for us to talk to each other.

---

145 Berger J (2015) 'Some Notes on Song'. *Harpers Magazine*.

Chapter 18: Rest in fleece

Death is anecdotal, a personal narrative attached to a particular living creature. We are alive or not alive. Statistics can only give me a general idea of where I am in the story. And while stemming the tide, any attempt to intervene in the overall scheme of things may be fruitless.

A large spider traverses the bath, makes fruitless attempts to climb up the side and slips back again. Struck by a wave of ecological sensitivity, my friend gathers it carefully in a tooth tumbler and deposits it on the windowsill. A spotted flycatcher swoops down and eats it for breakfast: so much for good intentions.

While there are a number of conversations we can have about death (dying, death itself, disposal and the grief of those left behind), it is very difficult to envisage the world without oneself. After all, if my 'self' is an illusion cooked up by the immune system, how about all you others? Are you real? Is it only me in which reality is a sleight of hand?

Perhaps it is only when we are dying that we shall be able to lay down the burden of projections and introjections that shape our perceptions and capacity for relationships – and contemplate a world that exists without our presence. In an act of courage and self-obliteration, the poet Dorothy Nimmo speaks from the brink of an unknown premise, 'After…' and then hesitates:

What words lie beyond 'after'?

Propped up by advances in technology, not only are we living longer but in Britain the population is soaring, with three million more mouths to feed by 2026[146]. Malthus was correct in his assertion that there would be, and are now, too many of us bed blockers; we are a drag on the economy. But it is not only consciousness of our superfluity that suggests to us it is time to move on. The run-up to death was aptly summed up by the filmstar Bette Davis, 'Old age ain't no place for sissies'. The aches and pains and slow deteriorations afflict heroes and sissies alike and we do not get a choice on timing: apart from the very few who simply drop dead, dying can be extended and unpleasant. My Aunt Phyll was one of the lucky ones. Oscillating between melancholy and good cheer, she lived in an oast house during the war and raised four piglets, 'Pork', 'Ham', 'Bacon' and 'Brawn'. In an optimistic if unexpected exit, she ordered a flamboyant poppy red car, test drove it, went to bed that evening and never woke up.

At present, there is much discussion about assisted dying, with frustration and indignation massaging statistics heavily on both sides of the ethical arguments. Since current law discourages us from making away with ourselves, the nearest we can get is to sign a 'Do Not Attempt Cardiopulmonary Resuscitation' form, discouraging the diligent from over the top restoration of the status quo, following a severe heart attack or stroke.

However, as I discovered the other day, the same question posed by an anaesthetist, when one is strapped to a trolley before being wheeled into

146 Webster B (2016) Public want action to curb rapid population growth. *The Times.* **10 October**

emergency surgery and moments before clamping down the mask of oblivion, takes on a more urgent quality. In spite of potential distraction offered by a Disney frieze of lions and giraffes queuing for the Ark, I found my attention focused acutely on the inexorable traverse of existence. The second hand swept on regardless, 'Nine, eight, seven, si…': Russian roulette with a DNACPR decision. The question is, who will chicken out during the countdown? Imminence really does focus the mind on the reality of termination: what if? What if nothing?

While my nerve held, a social psychologist friend suggested that I should have taken the opportunity to collect statistics entitled, 'Alterations in Perspective under Conditions of Stress' and held up my hand requesting a short pause. 'Hang on to the poised knife for a minute while I ascertain the proportion of those of us whose resolve cracks when faced with the possibility of imminent demise?'

One way or another life is full of car crashes, and death is always round the next corner. But this one is for real: middle of the night, coming round a bend, lights flash, brake, skid, sheer off tree, car tips over, thrown sideways, time suspended as my head traces an involuntary arc, hanging upside down, head dangling from safety belt in passenger foot-well: too fast for punctuation.

Even the left-brain interpreter is shocked into silence. Unable to move, I have ceded control: nothing I can do except wait. Undead; I've become an object to be manipulated by other than myself. Existential or not, what I am conscious of is emptiness.

This time however I'm not dead, it's a matter of bumps and bruises, although later inspection of the ripped scarf of bark hanging from the tree trunk suggests that a couple of inches to the right could have had a wrap-round definitive 'end-of' outcome.

Mathematical models assure us that we are all doomed. I think we all knew this anyway, even if we prefer not to dwell on it. Apart from accident and self-destruction, in biological terms either our cells gradually wither and are not replaced, so that we collapse from organ failure or dementia, or alternatively burst into cancerous malignancy. While I'm not sure which I prefer, one way or another we are all on our way out. And in some part, we are afraid, if not of being dead, of the process of dying.

Not this time: a face like a harvest moon appears at the window; hand reaches in and switches off the engine. Whether or not he is my guardian angel, a man wrenches open the back of the car and wriggles into the wreckage. Somehow he wedges his leg between the front seats and supports my shoulders – and sits there waiting with me. His kindness and presence take away fear. And when the fire crews arrive to extract me, he leaves. That's it: an encapsulate meeting with a good Samaritan called Dean who was on his way to Monmouth. I know nothing else about him.

The old do tend to dwell on death; it creeps around in the mind, popping up in unlikely contexts and spawning clichés, such as 'the trouble with death is that there is no future in it'. But sleeping in two-hour slots, uninterrupted dormancy is attractive; a desirable alternative to life on an hyperactive treadmill. Far from being depressed, and fascinating though life is, sometimes I've had enough.

Turning to the wider prospect of mortality, I respond to an invitation to a café discussion under the title, 'Death Café'. Difficult to break the ice on such a tricky subject but the convener rises to the occasion; 'Hands up those who are not going to die'. This is a rallying cry that commands instant attention. Eyes front, a random group of people collectively clicks its heels. Our wandering thoughts are now focused on a single issue. Whoever we are and whatever our interests, we are united by the inevitability of demise and ready to respond to this fusion of humour and demand. All ears open, we are ready to begin discussion.

The Death Café is a movement started in America with the intention of creating a forum for people to feel comfortable with talking about demise and so decreasing fear of death[147].

Rather than feeling uncomfortable with the idea of death, my initial reaction is that the name of the gathering itself is unfortunate, since it risks trivialising what is the most unequivocal event that will occur in our lifespan, certainly the most inevitable. And it sends out the wrong impression to those of us who live in this block of retirement homes. Most are women, ex-wives, predeceased by our husbands. A preliminary circular inviting residents to a 'Death Cafe' meeting is greeted with incredulity by widows in the sheltered living home, who feel they are deeply acquainted with the subject and do not require what they see as counselling by the well-meaning, and it is at best patronising, since we are the experts. But it turns out that Death Café is a discussion group, rather than support or counselling session. So why does this attempt to cosy up to extinction provoke such an outcry? I'm not convinced that it is fear which puts us off talking about our inevitable, but intrigued, I read the promotional literature:

'Stiff-upper-lipped Brits have a particular problem talking about death. Anyone who tries invariably gets shouted down with "Don't talk like that!" or superstitiously looking over one's shoulder, "If you say a grief, you'll make it happen". A survey by the charity 'Dying Matters' reveals that more than 70 per cent of us are uncomfortable talking about death and less than a third of us have spoken to family members about end-of life wishes. The pamphlet continues:

'At a Death Cafe people, often strangers, gather to eat cake, drink tea and discuss death.' The objective is 'to increase awareness of death with a view to helping people make the most of their (finite) lives'. A Death Café is a group directed discussion of death with no agenda, objectives or themes.

Death Cafe publicity all seems very wholesome, although while eating and drinking are seen as an essential part of social bonding in the face of terminal decline, an uncomfortable murmur in my brain points out that, while pleasurable, eating cake is about obesity and diabetes and hastening death. In my case there is an additional snag – a range of sensitivities relating to some amino acid present in tea, coffee, cheese and chocolate, all of which makes

---

147 Battersby M (2016) 'The Death Café Movement: Tea and Mortality' *The Independent* **27 August**

enthusiastic social participation in the slogan 'Eating is about living' tricky.
A shudder in the mirror suggests I already do too much of that.

All this is hearsay before I actually manage to attend a meeting of the
Death Café, which turns out to be an anti-climax, a gathering of seven
people sharing their sadness, more about life's shadows than death. So many
moving stories, which are not mine to tell but which echo in all our lives.
And yet, without disrespect, a piece of doggerel from the comedian Stanley
Holloway's recitation, 'Albert and the Lion', keeps popping up in my mind.
As a small boy Albert is taken to the seaside – but there are 'no wrecks and
nobody drowned, fact nothing to laugh at, at all'. Albert's family decide to
move on to the greater excitements of the zoo and a lion which, as far as
I remember, devours Albert including the stick that Albert has used to poke
the lion through the bars of its cage.

Oscillating between attempts to defend myself with humour and looking
straight ahead, I want to introduce a final testament from a woman who
died recently, Donna Williams. Donna, who had a long battle with metastic
cancer, has my profound admiration. Autistic and growing up in a totally
dysfunctional family (who describe her as 'the loony in the attic'), she offers
those of us who live on an extraordinary joy and celebration of living in her
perception of the transition to not living. At times she is almost ecstatic.

*'I am a Taoist. I fear no dark, it illuminated all that was bright and warm
and wonderful. I thank the dark for teaching me the value of light. Too many
people freeze in the headlights when faced with their own death or that of those
with whom they are close. Yet we all encounter these experiences. We might as
well empower ourselves, educate ourselves, familiarize ourselves, rid ourselves
of taboos, stereotypes, projections, mythologizing, presumptions of one-size-fits
all. Even if all one has are months, not years, there may still be life to be lived,
transitions to be made and these can be poignant, epic, warm, wondrous, even
beautiful.'*

*'We die. This is the one certainty of our lives. And for those who do not
believe in afterlife, I embrace the idea of treating death as transition and also,
of living on in the minds of those we have met and helped and loved. We are
part of the chain of being.'*[148]

One of the facets of our belief with which we all live is that of the present,
an illusion whose reality evades us, since by the time it takes to identify
current events in our left brain, they are already part of our past. Out of sync
with the present we live in retrospect. Perhaps when we die (since we shall
have left our interpreter in the ashes), in eternity we shall finally catch up
with and can participate in the present. Time will tell, or rather time may tell:
it is only the atheist who will know if they are wrong about the afterlife.

And for the believer, death itself should also not present a problem, since
it is not seen to be the end of conscious awareness, in what is promised to
be a 'better place'. Even if we are living 'as if', adopting a story that stands
somewhere between the oasis of belief and empty wastes of atheism (and
whether the direction of our search is neurological, philosophical or spiritual),

148 http://www.donnawilliams.net/384.0.html

we continue to reach beyond the death for the genesis of meaning. In respect of afterwards, if there is afterwards, eternity seems an awfully long time, especially as was pointed out at the death café, if one is to be accompanied by those with whom affection was not part of the relationship.

When it comes to disposal, we children had a cemetery for dead insects behind the school stable, home to Darkie, a pony rather too free with his rear hooves. We scraped beetle-sized graves in loose earth and decorated them with garlands of laburnum flowers. Our interest lasted about a week and then faded and, in the way that children move on so quickly, it was considered odd even to refer to our funereal episode. We had done burials and were now into climbing trees.

Looking at the dead, husband, father, sister, daughter, our deceased bodies are so different. They don't belong to us any more, at least there is no 'us' for them to belong to. The owner has sold up and left an uninhabited object, a thing.

Once we can get past the multitude of funeral plans insuring our loved ones against being crippled by the soaring costs of disposal, there are a number of alternatives open to dispatching our remains. Having one's ashes fired from the mouth of a canon into the ether for swift dispersal – smacks of ostentation, and runs the risk of being greeted at the pearly gates with the admonition against a final sin of showing off ('doesn't go down well up here'). Co-op Funeral Services are less flamboyant: for 50 pence a day ('before it is too late'), customers are invited to curate their own 'Stylish Funerals'.

A ceramicist friend who sent me a dish glazed with the glass from my fractured car window, suggests that after cremation in her own kiln she would like to use her ash to glaze her urn. She is evasive when I ask her what would then be inside but perhaps interiority and exteriority are meaningless concepts in the eternal scheme of things. 'Mother on the mantelpiece', cannot be contained inside her vase. But we warm to the idea of filling it with flowers.

Although there is a shortage of land space for burial, being returned to the earth seems more eco-friendly than reduction to ash that will not degrade. But does it matter for me since I am dead; just another run-out-of-time cadaver? While resistant to the innovative green idea of the liquefaction of my carcass (down the drain gets personal), what I should really like is a biodegradable coffin and swift entry into the food chain, biological recycling; remaining part of the order of things.

'Rest in Fleece' suggests that we wrap ourselves in woollen shrouds. In the 17th century an Act was passed act stipulating that all corpses must be buried in woollen shrouds. (Was it ever repealed?) Recently revived, 'sales of woollen coffins have grown by 700% as increasing numbers of Britons choose eco-funerals over traditional services.'[149]

Eschewing wicker (undertakers complain that it creaks when lifted or the hearse hits a pothole while they are driving, or somewhat alarmingly for the congregation, as the body settles on the bier during the funeral service),

---

149 Nugent H www.theguardian.com › Environment › Ethical and green living June 12 2012

an ecological alternative is made of sheep wool laced with recycled cardboard, 'independently tested and accredited for strength and weight'. Available in cream or black, with an embroidered nameplate, each coffin is made from three fleeces. Bellacouche offer a nice sideline in tea cosies[150]. Presumably left-overs from small corpses? ('We might get two out of this one?') How about a 'Knit and Natter', do it yourself knitting circle, 'knit one, pearl one and don't forget to cast off for the handles?'

Even conventional funerals have their own flavour. The only qualification to my father's interment in an ancient island churchyard is that it is dependent on the water table, which in its turn is reliant on the state of the tide and ultimately on lunar fluctuations. At high tide the coffin floats. So the timing of funerals in parts of the churchyard is critical and determined by tide tables.

The family assemble on a bright sunny day at low tide. My cousin Tim, who is six foot ten and massive with it, teeters perilously over a drainage ditch on a fragile plank to the graveside muttering, 'This is the sort of bridge that makes one feel one should seriously diet before attempting a crossing'. After the ceremony, the child of a friend comes running down the lane, her face full of excitement. 'Was it a lovely funeral?' We agree that it was.

Black humour is a slightly dubious guest at funerals, a temporary defence against grief. Everyone has favourite disposal stories. Asked to escort the ashes of a colleague home from a European Conference, a colleague of my husband was left standing on the platform at the Swiss border in his pyjamas, after getting off the train to sign the customs paperwork in the middle of the night. The ashes travelled on to London unaccompanied.

Scattering ashes is all very well, if one knows exactly where they should be released (unless one opts for the unlikely solution of dumping them in the stratosphere). But my sister had waved a hand vaguely in the general direction of a wood that turned out to be owned by an extremely possessive land owner, so the family was reduced to sneaking in furtively through a hole in the hedge before he appeared and told us to go elsewhere. I still feel guilty that I was unable to organise a more dignified disposal. Burial at sea, is accompanied by the hazard of an unanticipated breeze puffing spicules of bone back into one's hair.

Disposal is fraught with euphemisms. Fused into jewellery, ashes of the departed can be perpetuated, 'hand-crafted in our specialist glass workshops'[151].

Your loved one's cremation ashes, colored glass crystals and clear molten glass are expertly layered together to create a beautiful, lasting tribute to the one you hold dear. Your 'Ashes into Glass' jewelry will remind you that your loved one is with you. Each 'Ashes into Glass' stone is unique and, just like your loved one, will possess its own character.'

One can imagine circumstances that might demand two or three alternatives to reflect different facets of the beloved's character? Opal, ruby, jet black?

---

150 bellacouche.com/product-category/bellacouche-shop/

151 Ashes into Glass Jewellery is hand-crafted by James Watts, Bill Rhodes and their team at Barleylands Glassworks in Billericay, Essex. (accessed April 2019)

'It may remind you of a starry night's sky, a wispy cloud. By wearing it or just holding it in your hand, you will connect with your loved one and share these special moments together.' Maybe Mum and Dad rings, worn on separate hands – they never really got on with each other? Although the jewelry is handsome, the prose grates. Dubious taste crystallises: 'the cremation ashes glass piglet paperweight?'[152].

But more importantly, human grief involves letting go both of positive and negative memories. However tender, like listening to a message from the grave, caressing a lump of glass could be a bridge but is just as likely to recall absence. Fixing the remains of one's beloved in pin-down jewellery turns them into an object that can be manipulated and hinders internalisation. How can we rebuild life, while a swirl of one's departed is holding down a pile of unpaid bills? Poor fly trapped in amber: fascination trembles on the border of obsession. Better flowers that fade. Let me go when I'm gone: extending my physical presence in an ornament seems to undervalue my part in the cycle of life and death and the natural world of which I am part.

The options are endless, the latest 'Resomation' whereby the body is liquefied, which carries the advantage that artificial joints can be recycled. Or possibly donating one's body to a hospital for teaching purposes – together with the humiliating possibility of ultimate rejection as one misses out on their requirements: no cancer, no HIV and no post-mortem, the latter presumably interfering with dissection.

Curiously enough, although in my student days I enjoyed and was good at dissection, I confess to some resistance to the idea of my body being the subject of the knife and such intimate exploration at the hands of an unknown medical student. Nevertheless, the aim is admirable, even if much of the surgeon's training can now be virtual; although the hazards of the 'surgical smoke plume' – whereby trainees using a laser or electrosurgical unit may be exposed to gases such as benzene, hydrogen cyanide, formaldehyde and other nasty products generated by what is known as 'target tissues' – suggest that this hands-on teaching approach remains to be perfected.

However, reduced to the anonymity of a cadaver, I shall consider whether I can overcome my squeamishness and the possibility of bodily donation to science. How about my brain in a bottle, even if the marbles rattle when you shake it?

Grief is not so easily disposed of. The loves in our lives die and we are dismantled by pain, taken apart as we learn the meaning of never. Sylvia Plath's poem 'Widow' opens with a stanza that, nearly 50 years on, strips the dressing from a near mortal wound.

Widow. The word consumes itself –
Body, a sheet of newsprint on the fire
Levitating a numb minute in the updraft

152 Bathaquaglass: http://www.bathaquaglass.com/all-cremation-glass-products/ashes-glass-paperweight.html

Over the scalding red topography
That will put her heart out like an only eye.[153]

Mist on the surface of a mirror, breathing is the distinction between life and death. In the most powerful metaphor of all, we are 'uttered', 'whispered', 'spoken', 'told': at the climax of an exquisite setting of the second creation story by Aaron Copeland, 'In The Beginning', 'God breaths into man's nostrils and man becomes a living soul'[154].

Let us have some dignity and a gathering of friends at our end, since even if we are absent, the core, the quiddity of our spirit lives on in affective ripples lapping the lives of family and those we love. We leave an affective thumbprint on our circle of contacts.

Meanwhile there is grief left behind. A friend who knows sadness sends me the sonnet 'Funeral Prayer', by Don Paterson, and says, 'Poetry can sing its way through lives of sorrow, grief and joy. It holds both spirituality and the sense of the common sharing of humanity.'

Over but not quite out. Dying drags its heels[155]. Even after our breath has ceased to cloud the glass, the brain has rattled its last marble and the heart no longer beats, our immune system goes on fighting a frenzied rearguard action to the last white blood corpuscle left standing...

Maybugs, you die stranded on your back, clawing the air when your dwindling nervous system can no longer sustain the necessary motor signals telling your legs to keep walking. I hope when it comes to the end of my lifecycle, someone will close my eyes and cross my arms across my breast. It seems more dignified.

153 Reproduced with permission of Faber and Faber Ltd.

154 Aaron Copeland 'In the Beginning'. A cappella with mezzo-soprano soloist based on the Genesis Second Creation Story

155 Guigo R (2018) The effects of death and post-mortem cold ischemia on human tissue transcriptomes *Nature Communications* **volume 9**.

Coda

Looking back through the chapters of *Maybugs and Mortality*, I ask myself what has been the point of this tandem excursion? I still know what I knew at the beginning: that we are born, we live, that we die. But Maybug's publicity-seeking cousin the scarab has his photo in *The Times* the other day. There he is, nestling among the hieroglyphs in an illustration taken from the *Book of the Dead*. I recognise Ammit first, the nasty looking creature in the bottom right hand corner, crocodile head, leopard torso and hippo rump, waiting to gobble up any heart that is 'heavy with the weight of any wrongdoing'[156]. The ostrich plume from the hat of Maat weighing in on the opposite scale of balance clinches it: we are in the Judgement Hall, looking at the ceremonial judgement of the heart after death in ancient Egypt. Watched by Osiris, the proceedings are being adjudicated by a jury of deities and recorded by the scribe Thoth, writing on a scroll of papyrus. And yes, Scarab, you are represented in your capacity to act as a witness (sometimes false witness), to the deceased's purity; talisman and passport to heaven. An accompanying article describes the advent of new technologies that will make it possible to decipher scrolls that have been charred by fire. Too fragile to unroll, they are as yet unread. So much more to be learned.

Maybugs, you have led me an odd cultural dance. Had we not met, I should have had absolutely no idea what this picture was about and should never have found out that I share a pack of genes with the tree outside my window.

And from the point of view of my limited understanding, some insects have moved up a notch on the scale of consciousness. I still don't know quite where Maybugs sits on the affective scale. First cousin to a God, does she have any sense of herself and what she is doing? But from my standpoint, what I notice overall is an intimacy shift in myself from the formal towards the more personal, from 'Melolontha' and 'Cockchafer', to 'The Maybug', or even adopting 'Maybugs' as her name, so that now in my mind, I may address her as, 'Hi there, Maybugs', someone I can greet. Skirting the danger that familiarity can pave the path to anthropomorphism, I have eased my way from the formality of 'du' to 'tu', to respect rather than distaste.

We are both players and audience in our lives. What makes being alive such a ride is curiosity and the potential flowering of relationships. And now I understand a little bit more about one of my fellow travellers.

Till has the last laugh. Emailed to an academic colleague for comment with subject abbreviated to, 'Bugs and Me', this draft was rejected by her university server, but accepted when resent as, 'A Single Case Study of the effects of Aging in Melolontha Melolontha. J. Geriatrica Vol 1 pp 1-114.

---

156 http://www.egyptian-scarabs.co.uk/weighing_of_the_heart.htm